P9-BHS-837

UNDERSTANDING WHITETAILS

By Dr. Dave Samuel

Dr. David Samuel, a Professor of Wildlife Biology at West Virginia University, began hunting whitetails with bow and arrow over 40 years ago. He serves as Conservation Editor for Bowhunter Magazine and is on the board of directors of the Pope and Young Club.

CY DECOSSE INCORPORATED

Creative Publishing
A Division of Cowles Enthusiast Media

President/COO: Nino Tarantino
Executive V.P./Editor-in-Chief: William B. Jones

UNDERSTANDING WHITETAILS
By Dr. David Samuel

Executive Editor, Outdoor Products Group: Don Oster
Contributing Writer and Book Development Leader: David R. Maas
Editors: Chris Madson, Ron Spomer
Senior Editor: Bryan Trandem
Technical Editors/Advisors: Dave Canfield, M. R. James - Bowhunter Magazine
Managing Editor: Denise Bornhausen
Copy Editor: Janice Cauley
Associate Creative Director: Brad Springer
Senior Art Director: Dave Schelitzche
Senior Desktop Publishing Specialist: Joe Fahey
Desktop Publishing Specialist: Laurie Kristensen
V.P. Photography and Production: Jim Bindas
Studio Manager: Marcia Chambers
Staff Photographers: Mike Hehner, William Lindner
Photo Assistants: Thomas Heck, David Tieszen
Photo Editor: Anne Price
Production Manager: Stasia Dorn
Production Staff: Dave Austad, Laura Hokkanen, Tom Hoops, Mike Schauer
Illustrator: Dave Schelitzche
Cover Photo (The Complete Hunter): Charles J. Alsheimer
Cover Photo (The Complete Bowhunter): Bill Lea

Enthusiast Media

President/COO: Philip L. Penny

Contributing Photographers: Charles J. Alsheimer, Mike Biggs, Denver Bryan, Gary Clancy, Daniel J. Cox, Jeanne Drake, J. Faircloth, D. Robert Franz, The Green Agency, Donald M. Jones, Bill Kinney, Lance Krueger, Claudine Laabs, Lon E. Lauber, Bill Lea, Steve Maas, Bill Marchel, Minnesota Historical Society, Janice Ozoga, Tim Peterson, Ted Rose, Daniel Snyder, Bob Zaiglin

Cooperating Individuals, Agencies and Manufacturers: ALS Enterprises/Scent-Lok - Jim Hill; Browning - Paul Thompson; Chris Gulden; Eric Lindberg; Lohman Mfg. Company, Inc. - Brad Harris; Mississippi State University - Harry A. Jacobson; Mountaineer Archery - Pat Nealis; Northern Sun Outdoor Group, Inc./Backland - Scott Anderson, John Ozoga; Pope and Young Club - Glenn E. Hisey; Predator, Inc. - Marc Barger; Scientific Hunters Division/Information Outfitters, Inc. - Michael Leary; Spartan Realtree - Dodd Clifton, Bill Jordan; Stephen F. Austin State University - Dr. James C. Kroll; Pat and Tom Wagamon

Printing: R. R. Donnelley & Sons Co. (1096)
99 98 97 96 / 5 4 3 2 1

Copyright © 1996 by Cowles Creative Publishing
5900 Green Oak Drive
Minnetonka, MN 55343
1-800-328-3895

The Library of Congress has cataloged The Complete Bowhunter edition as follows:

Samuel, David (David Evan)
Understanding Whitetails/by David Samuel.
p. cm. - (The Complete Bowhunter)
Includes index.
ISBN 0-86573-069-5 (hardcover).
1. White-tailed deer hunting. 2. White-tailed deer.
I. Title. II. Series.
SK301.5218 1996   96-25979
799.2'77357--dc20

Contents

Introduction

The whitetail deer *(Odocoileus virginianus)* is the most widely distributed and abundant big game animal in North America. Whitetails have evolved to survive in a wide variety of habitats; from dry, arid regions of Texas to wetlands of Louisiana; from mountain forests of Montana to suburbs of Chicago. Their North American population is estimated at over 20 million.

Over 15 million hunters annually harvest about 4 million whitetails. These hunters spend billions of dollars each year on food, lodging, travel, equipment and licenses. In addition to countless days of outdoor recreation, hunters are rewarded with excellent-tasting venison, which is lower in fat and calories than beef.

Nonhunters also spend a great deal of money observing, photographing and appreciating whitetails. One study showed the combined value of whitetails to hunters and nonhunters in the United States was $27.3 billion, making it the most important wild mammal in America.

Understanding Whitetails is written specifically for hunters who pursue whitetails with bow and arrow, but it will be enjoyed by anyone with the desire to learn more about this magnificent species. Detailed illustrations, graphs, charts and beautiful full-color photos will help you understand every aspect of a deer's life.

In the first section, "Whitetail Basics," you'll learn where the 30 different whitetail subspecies are found, how to age a deer by examining its teeth, where the scent glands are located and how to fool a whitetail's eyes, ears and nose.

"Whitetail Populations & Habitats" covers the history of deer numbers in North America from before Europeans settled the continent to the present. You'll also see where deer densities are highest and lowest in the United States and learn how particular habitats affect deer differently through the seasons.

In "Whitetail Behavior" you'll find out which foods are preferred in various habitats, how deer communicate visually and vocally, when whitetails form into social groups and how individual animals assert dominance over others. This section also explains how you can take advantage of deer movement and the various stages of the breeding season to be a more effective hunter.

The final section, "Trophy Bucks," shows you what factors affect the size of a buck's antlers and how to improve deer habitat and manage a deer herd. You'll also learn the top ten places in North America to find a buck with record-book-size antlers.

And for the hunter wishing to harvest such an animal, he or she must first learn how to quickly and accurately field-judge a deer's rack. "Trophy Bucks" teaches you this process by providing detailed photographs of bucks viewed from several angles.

This book will help you be more successful in the field whether you carry a bow and arrow, camera or binoculars. Perhaps the most satisfying outdoor experience is unraveling the daily movement patterns and habits of the whitetails in your area, and then entering their world to observe them at distances of only a few yards. *Understanding Whitetails* gives you the knowledge to make this possible.

— *Dr. Dave Samuel*

Whitetail Basics

Whitetail buck crossing river, and doe with bur-filled coat (inset)

Whitetail Characteristics

If success is measured in years, our common white-tail is a superstar. For more than 4 million years, it has been evolving, adapting and thriving in North America. From the bitter snows of the north woods to the noisy suburbs of our southern cities, whitetails eat, sleep and breed, filling fields and woods with animated beauty. Highly specialized physical characteristics enable them to avoid predators, tolerate numerous habitats, eat a wide variety of vegetation and survive temperature extremes.

Appropriately, the whitetail is named for the conspicuous underside of its wide tail, which it often raises, or *flags* (p. 49), when alarmed. Males, called *bucks,* grow antlers during late spring and summer and shed them in winter. Unlike mule and blacktail deer antlers, which usually fork (opposite page), a whitetail's antlers branch into individual points growing from a continuous main beam. Females, called *does,* rarely grow antlers.

Biologists have identified 30 whitetail subspecies in North and Central America (opposite page). While all share the same general characteristics, each is slightly different in pelage tint and pattern, body size and proportion, and range. These slight differences are adaptations to regional conditions.

O. v. leucurus

O. v. dacotensis

O. v. ochrourus

O. v. couesi

O. v. texanus

O. v. carminsis

O. v. sinaloae

O. v. acapulcensis

O. v. mexicanus

O. v. oaxacensis

O. v. toltecus

O. v. thomasi

O. v. nelsoni

O. v. mcilhennyi

O. v. miquihuanensis

O. v. veraecrucis

O. v. nemoralis

O. v. rothschildi

O. v. borealis

O. v. macrourus

O. v. virginianus

O. v. taurinsulae

O. v. venatorius

O. v. hiltonensis

O. v. nigribarbis

O. v. osceola

O. v. seminolus

O. v. clavium

O. v. yucatanensis

O. v. chiriquensis

Whitetail deer (Odocoileus virginianus) subspecies in North and Central America

How to Identify Mule Deer and Blacktail Deer

MULE DEER (left) are named for their very large, mulelike ears. Muleys have a large, white rump patch and a small, tube-shaped tail, which is white with a black tip. Bucks typically have antlers with forked main beams and small brow tines. Their racks are often wider and taller than those of whitetails.

BLACKTAIL DEER (right) are closely related to mule deer, but they have a smaller white rump patch and a flat tail, which is dark brown or black on the outside. Blacktail bucks usually have smaller antlers than those of whitetails or mule deer.

Seasonal Changes in a Whitetail's Coat

Reddish brown summer coat

Shedding the summer coat

Grayish brown winter coat

Agile and quick, whitetails are designed to escape predators in woodland environments by leaping (they can clear 8-foot fences), dodging and running through heavy cover at 25 mph. In the open, they've been clocked galloping nearly 40 mph – an elusive meal for the hungriest wolf.

Because they never know when the next predator might attack, whitetails are always alert and ready to flee, but they stay on their toes for another reason, too. Each of their slender feet is tipped with a pair of 3-inch-long hooved toes made of *keratin,* a hornlike substance similar to that of fingernails. Although there are two shorter toes called *dewclaws* (above) just behind and above the main hooves, these don't normally touch the ground unless a deer is running or in soft mud. Essentially, deer walk on their tiptoes. Front hooves are slightly longer than rear hooves.

Because most whitetails must adapt to temperature extremes, they produce seasonal wardrobes (left). An adult deer grows a thin, reddish brown jacket for hot summer climates and a thick, grayish brown coat to insulate against winter cold. The winter coat has long guard hairs and short, dense, insulating underfur so efficient that snow can settle on it without melting.

Secretions produced by skin glands make the coat water-repellent and keep frigid rain or lake water from penetrating to the skin (right). Throughout much of North America, deer *molt* (lose their summer pelage and grow their winter coat) in August or September.

Hair not only protects whitetails from weather, but, because of its dull color, also camouflages them from sharp-eyed predators. Coat color varies slightly in different parts of the country, tending to be darker

NEWBORN WHITETAILS, called *fawns*, have coats with 270 to 340 white spots over a brown background. This contrasting color pattern enables fawns to blend in with the light and dark patterns of sun and shade to avoid detection by predators.

in forested areas of the East and lighter in the open, dry West. In the tropics, whitetail pelts are redder and blacker. Regardless of where they live, all have white hair on their belly, chin and neck; around eyes and nose; and, of course, under that famous tail.

Melanism (black pigmentation) and *albinism* (white pigmentation) in deer are rare. However, there is a seven-county area in central Texas where 8 to 9 percent of the deer are melanistic. In parts of two of these counties, the incidence runs as high as 21 percent. Another rare condition is *piebald* coloration – white blotches scattered randomly amid a normally tinted pelage.

Albino whitetail

11

Aging Whitetails by the Tooth-Wear-and-Replacement Technique

When deer are born, they have three milk teeth on each side of their lower jaw. In less than 2 years, the milk teeth are pushed out and replaced by three permanent premolars. Three additional molars sprout behind these, giving adult deer a total of six teeth on each side of the lower jaw. By knowing when this tooth replacement occurs, you can estimate the age of a deer.

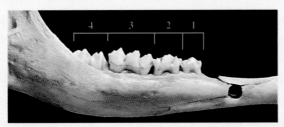

To use the tooth-wear-and-replacement method, start by examining one-half of the lower jaw of a deer. If the jaw has fewer than six teeth (above), the deer is no more than 1 year old.

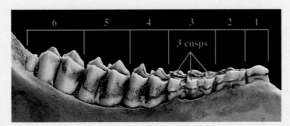

If the jaw has six teeth, you must examine the third tooth from the front. If this tooth has three cusps, or points, it's a milk tooth and the deer is 17 or 18 months old (above). If the third tooth has two cusps, it is a permanent premolar (having replaced a milk tooth) and the deer is at least 19 months old.

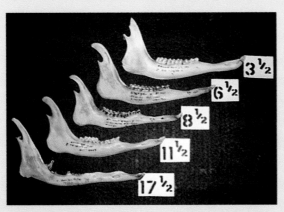

In this case, to more precisely determine the deer's age, you must examine the wear on the cusps of the three molars. Unfortunately, tooth wear varies widely, depending on diet. As a result, the deer's age can only be approximated to plus or minus 1 year. Very old deer usually have severely worn molars (above).

Age & Growth

AGE – Though deer up to 10 years of age are killed by automobiles and hunters in most states and provinces each year, the majority of whitetails do not live beyond 4 or 5 years. In areas where hunting pressure is extreme, like most of the eastern states, about 70 percent of deer taken are 1½ years old. Normally, does live more than twice as long as bucks because the males burn up their fat reserves and often seriously injure one another during the breeding season. When winter snow and cold hit, they are often too weak to find sufficient food.

Old whitetails, especially bucks, are larger and bulkier than young deer, and their antlers are usually larger. The number of tines, however, does not indicate age. The most accurate way to determine a deer's age is to get it right from the horse's mouth, so to speak. Field biologists commonly "age" whitetails by examining their teeth for wear and replacement (left). Biologists can also age deer by slicing a thin cross section of the root of an incisor tooth with a tiny saw, then examining with a microscope the layers of annuli (similar to counting the rings of a tree).

Growth of Whitetails in Texas

Age	**Bucks** (pounds)	**Does** (pounds)
6 months	50	50
1½ years	70	60
2½ years	92	68
3½ years	102	74
4½ years	110	78
5½ years	111	78
6½ years	109	77
7½ years	99	71

THE AVERAGE FIELD-DRESSED WEIGHT (in pounds) of bucks and does of different ages is shown above. Notice that both sexes grew to maximum size in 5½ years, then lost weight by age 7½.

Full-grown Canada and Florida Keys (inset) whitetails

GROWTH – At birth, fawns weigh from 4 to 8 pounds. In 4 to 5 years, they are full grown, standing about 3 feet at the shoulder and measuring 5 to 6 feet from sensitive black nose to flicking white tail. Adult bucks weigh about 25 to 30 percent more than adult does, but this can vary greatly, depending on habitat type. For instance, in the northern and midwestern United States and Canada, bucks commonly weigh twice as much as does.

Across much of the whitetail's range, bucks average 100 to 150 pounds, but northern deer are much heavier than southern deer. For example, large bucks from Canada can weigh 300 pounds (above), while the tiny, endangered Florida Keys deer (inset above) might hit 50 pounds after a big meal. Many mammals and birds exhibit this phenomenon, known as *Bergman's Rule,* which states that individuals of a species living in cold climates will evolve a larger body size than those in warm climates. This increases their thermal efficiency, since large-bodied animals have less surface area relative to overall mass than do small-bodied animals. In other words, big deer more efficiently conserve body heat and have a better chance of surviving long, harsh winters.

Neither size nor weight are consistent from deer to deer in any region. Genetics can produce significantly different-sized deer within the same herd. Local forage production can boost or hinder weight gain, and overcrowding can lead to overbrowsing, poor nutrition and scrawny deer.

Weights also vary within the year. Bucks lose weight during the rut as they focus on finding and breeding females rather than on feeding. In the North,  both sexes lose about 20 percent of their body weight during winter. This occurs even among captive deer that receive all the food they can eat. Though such weight loss is normal, severe winters can lead to significant die-offs from malnutrition (above).

Body condition at the start of winter is important not only for survival, but also for production the following spring. A doe that is fat and healthy in late November has the best chance of producing a bouncing spotted fawn – or two – the following May. Similarly, a buck that steps into the first snows of winter in good health has a good chance of not only pulling through that hungry season, but also of growing a big rack the next spring.

Antlers

The cycle of antler growth among whitetail bucks is driven by the sun. In spring (April in the South and May in the North), longer days lead to an increase in the male hormone testosterone, which stimulates the growth of new antlers (photo 1). Antlers are bone, and they grow from the *pedicels*, specialized areas on the frontal bone that respond to testosterone. The pedicels, which get about ½ inch long, form when bucks are only 4 months old. These male fawns do not grow antlers during their first fall and are referred to as "button bucks." Some research suggests that the pedicels grow sooner in heavier, healthier fawns and later in fawns on poorer diets. Thus, it is probable that older bucks that are well fed start growing their antlers earlier than bucks that aren't getting enough high-quality forage.

While the antler itself is mostly nonliving calcium, the tissue that builds the antler is alive with many blood vessels and nerves covered by skin and soft hair. It's called "velvet." During early growth, the velvet and the antler forming inside it are mostly water. The rest of the tissue is 80 percent protein. For maximum antler growth, high-protein foods are needed about a month prior to the start of antler development.

Velvet is relatively soft, and it can be injured. Such damage can lead to a deformed antler. If there is an injury to the pedicel during early antler growth, a third antler or extra tines from the base of the antler may form. Damage later on in the antler's development may produce lumps or extra tines – such antlers are called *non-typical* (opposite page). Non-typical antlers can also result from a genetic quirk or body deformities. Studies show that deer with injured legs tend to have non-typical antlers. Interestingly, the non-typical antler is on the opposite side from the deformed limb. Thus, if a deer has an injured right front leg, the left antler may be deformed.

As the antlers continue to grow, the points begin to take shape along the main beam (photo 2). The antlers are still covered in velvet when they reach full size by the end of summer (photo 3).

As the days get shorter in early fall (August or September in the North and September or October in the South), continued high levels of testosterone cause the outer surface of the antler to harden. The antlers are now made up of 60 percent mineral and 40 percent organic matter. Once the antlers have hardened completely, the velvet dries up and either falls off (photo 4) or is rubbed off on saplings. Most

Buck with large non-typical antlers

of the velvet is shed in a day, but small pieces may remain on the antler for up to a week. Healthy bucks tend to shed velvet earlier than bucks in poor health.

By mid-fall the buck has polished his antlers by rubbing them on trees and brush (photo 5). The antlers are used in sparring during this time, and bucks often break off tines or portions of the main beam.

In mid- to late winter (December to March in the North; February to April in the South), a decrease in testosterone leads to antler shedding (photo 6). Healthy bucks tend to shed their antlers later than bucks in poor health. Usually both antlers do not drop off at the same time, but it is common to find both shed antlers within 100 yards of each other. This is probably the result of the buck feeling uncomfortable after one antler drops. The slight weight imbalance may cause him to shake his head, or brush against a tree, in an attempt to shake the second antler loose.

Antler velvet and hardened antlers have been used medicinally, especially in the Orient, for thousands of years. The uses vary, but some people believe that the velvet strengthens human bones and muscles. This use has led to a major industry of raising animals in captivity for "harvest" of the antlers and velvet. It also has led to the poaching of antlered animals in the wild.

Shed Antlers

As the interest in trophy bucks has grown, so has the "sport" of hunting shed antlers. Hunting "sheds" is a way to scout the area you plan to hunt the following fall.

The best time to hunt sheds is January to March. If you live in a part of whitetail country that gets a lot of snow, you have a built-in advantage. As snow deepens, deer tend to concentrate. This means that bucks are often confined to a small area when they drop their antlers, which makes shed hunting easier. Once the snow melts, hit the woods as soon as possible. The melting snow may leave open areas, where sheds are easily visible against the brown forest floor.

Looking for shed antlers is a lot like looking for deer. If you get snow in your area, use it to identify main trails from feeding areas to bedding areas. Once you have found these main trails and know where deer feed and bed during the winter, you have the keys for finding sheds. During the night, when bucks take a break from feeding, they sometimes bed in small ravines just inside the edges of woods adjacent to feeding fields. Check these areas for sheds. Then follow the main trails to the daytime bedding areas. Often, bucks drop their antlers either along these trails or in the bedding areas. Do not be concerned about disturbing these bedding areas, since it will be many months before hunting season begins.

One reason that shed hunting is so much more popular in the Midwest than in the East is because there are so many more large antlers to be found in that area. Smaller antlers are not only more difficult to see and find, they are also more quickly consumed by rodents. Larger sheds survive longer in nature and are a prize for any trophy hunter.

Shed hunting is a form of trophy hunting. Some hunters have found the sheds of a specific buck for 2 to 3 years before harvesting that buck during the hunting season. The search for those sheds provided clues to that buck's habits and behavior, and helped lead to his demise.

Whitetail scent glands

Scent Glands

Deer have at least seven external glands. Most secrete strongly scented liquids used to communicate with other deer.

The gland most familiar to hunters is the *tarsal gland* (right), located on the inner surface of the hind leg (most hunters call this area the "hock"). During the rut, bucks and does urinate on these glands while rubbing them together (called *rub-urination*). Rub-urination is a very

conspicuous scent-marking behavior. During the rut, this large gland is stained darker than the surrounding hair and is visible. The tarsal gland secretes lipids that interact with urine to produce odor that probably functions as a sexual attractant and/or to communicate dominance.

A 1995 study suggests that the odor produced from the combination of urine, tarsal gland, hair and bacteria varies for each deer. Thus, scent from this gland identifies individuals. Both sexes of all ages rub-urinate throughout the year, but in the few weeks prior to the peak of breeding, bucks will frequently exhibit this behavior while establishing and visiting scrapes (p. 72).

The *metatarsal gland* (right) is on the outer side of the lower hind leg. This gland is about 1½ inches long and is more prominent in northern white-tails than in their southern

Laying a Tarsal Gland Scent Trail

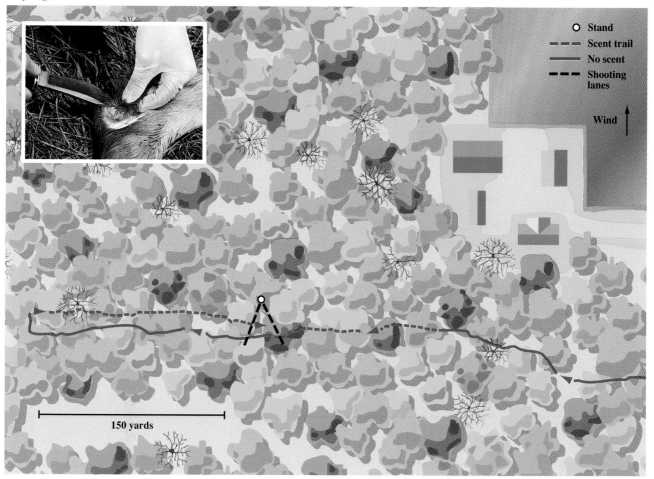

Stand ○
Scent trail – – –
No scent —
Shooting lanes ▬ ▬

Wind ↑

150 yards

CUT the tarsal gland (inset) from a rutting buck, and tie it to a piece of twine. After saturating the gland with doe-in-estrus scent, drag the tarsal to lure bucks into shooting range. Begin each scent line about 150 yards away from your stand, and continue until you've passed through your upwind shooting lanes.

cousins. Little is known about its function, but one researcher suggested that this gland may assist deer in controlling body heat (thermoregulation).

Small *interdigital glands* (right) between the hooves secrete a trail-marking odor. Some deer experts believe that fawns are protected from predators because they do not yet produce interdigital gland odor.

The *preorbital gland* (right) is a slit just in front of the corner of the eye. This tear duct gland has not been studied in whitetails, but dominant red deer stags have more visible gland openings than submissive deer. Thus, this gland probably functions during social interactions.

The *forehead gland* (right) is located between the eyes and antlers and has a lot to do with territoriality and mating. Bucks mark trees and limbs with this gland, and such markers become a focus for deer interactions.

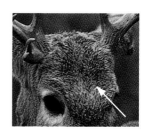

For years it was assumed that deer only used their antlers to rub trees. However, in recent years, researchers have found that, during the rut, whitetail bucks also commonly rub their foreheads on trees. Gland activity is highest in the most dominant bucks; thus, this gland is especially important in territory and dominance communication. The female whitetail also has forehead glands, but they produce much less scent than the glands of bucks.

Nasal glands probably function to lubricate the nose. They are found just inside the nostril. The *preputial gland* is found on the penis, but its function remains unknown.

Whitetail rotating its ear to pinpoint sounds

Senses

The whitetail is a deer of brush-land and forest. Its senses have evolved over millions of years to protect it in these environments. Its vision is acute, but the whitetail excels at hearing and smelling danger long before it can be seen in this dense habitat.

Hearing

Whitetails have large ears that collect the slightest abnormal sounds and funnel them to the brain for analysis. Background noise or danger? Falling nut or approaching predator? Common sounds not associated with danger – such as squirrels digging, traffic on a busy highway, people hiking a popular trail, barking dogs at a nearby country house – are ignored. But alien sounds, such as a body pushing through brush or an arrow squeaking against a bow, are recognized instantly as dangerous. Usually deer attempt to confirm a strange sound by seeing or smelling something out of place or at least hearing the same sound a second time, but heavily hunted whitetails vanish after just one false noise.

Whitetails owe their superior hearing to a pair of long ears, each of which forms a concave interior designed to catch and funnel sound to the inner ear. Each ear twists independently; thus, a deer can turn one ear forward and the other backward to listen for danger both ahead and behind. Once it hears something suspicious, it turns its eyes, nose and both ears to the source to confirm any potential danger. It can pinpoint the source of a sound from hundreds of yards away, particularly low frequencies, such as other deer grunting.

Tips for Fooling the Whitetail's Ears

CHOOSE clothing made of fabrics that are quiet, such as cotton, wool or fleece.

WEAR soft, rubber-soled boots to detect and avoid brittle branches, which will snap loudly if stepped on.

RATTLE antlers or blow a deer call to fool whitetails into thinking other deer are in the area. Antlers crashing are sounds that deer hear fairly often during the fall. In fact, many times a doe will feed in rather close proximity to fighting bucks. Hunters that rattle and call may not always attract deer, but they will almost never scare them.

level. Hot, dry air dissipates odors quickly, and rising currents carry them up and away.

In addition to "nosing out" food and predators, bucks identify and track other deer by scent. Does use smell to maintain contact with their fawns and to attract males. Various deer glands produce odors that communicate information about sex, their social position and, perhaps, scents indicating alarm.

Scent is critical during all phases of reproduction. During the summer, bucks communicate with each other by licking certain branches. These may be overhanging branches, but they also lick small, dead saplings. These saplings are usually 1 to 2 feet high, with no branches on them. Many bucks may visit the same licking branch during the year.

Bucks and does rub their forehead gland on buck rubs, sending messages of dominance to other deer (below). They also visit and urinate in scrapes. Bucks urinate over their tarsal glands, while does urinate directly into the scrape. The resulting odors and the messages they communicate are complex and may never be fully understood by humans. Once

Buck testing the wind for odors

Smell

A deer's sense of smell is its crowning glory. You might fool its eyes with camouflage and its ears with imitation calls, but if it catches one whiff of human odor, the game's over. By comparison, humans are "scent-deaf." We cannot begin to appreciate the talents of a whitetail's nose. But we can learn to respect them.

Because they spend so much time in heavy cover, whitetails must depend on their nose to keep them out of danger. The size of their prominent, black nose is indication of that. On damp days, they are at the peak of their olfactory powers. Moisture preserves odors, and cool air holds them near ground

Whitetail rubbing his forehead gland on a buck rub

a dominant buck determines that a doe is in estrus, he will form a "tending bond," and every 10 minutes or so, will approach the feeding doe and test her readiness. The female's scent often attracts a second or third buck. It is at this time that fights between bucks can, and do, occur.

Tips for Fooling the Whitetail's Nose

WEAR a carbon-lined Scent-Lok suit (above) under your outermost layer of hunting clothes to absorb odors. Wash your clothing in scent-free detergents, and store it in unscented plastic bags or a clean cooler until you are ready to hunt.

AVOID contaminating your clothes and body with strong odors from smoking cigarettes or pumping gas (above). Don't wear your camouflage clothes for the drive to and from your hunting area; instead, have a coverall suit used specifically for driving.

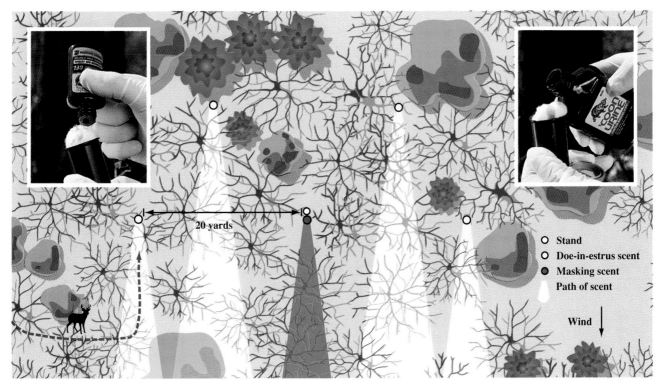

PLACE doe-in-estrus urine crosswind and upwind of your stand at a distance of about 20 yards. This often attracts bucks looking for a doe to breed. Put the scent on cotton balls held in plastic film canisters (left inset). Soak an additional cotton ball in a masking scent such as raccoon urine (right inset), and keep it at your stand.

Buck and doe traveling after dark

Sight

Deer have eyes on the sides of the head, which allows them to see in almost a complete circle without moving. Their daytime eyesight is very good; nighttime vision, excellent. Movement is easily detected by deer, but they apparently cannot pick out detail as well as humans, probably due to poorer overall depth perception.

Deer have evolved by being active during times when there is low light (above). This requires them to have exceptional night vision. They have a large eye, and a pupil that opens very wide. In fact, their pupil gathers about nine times more light than a human's pupil. Deer, and other nocturnal mammals, have a *tapetum lucidum*. This membrane reflects light through the retina a second time, thus enhancing night vision. You can see this in action by shining a light on a deer at night (right).

Deer also can see light in the *ultraviolet* portion of the spectrum. Ultraviolet is the very low portion of the spectrum, not visible to humans. This allows whitetails to see thousands of times better than humans at night.

The real question, the one asked by hunters over and over again, is, can deer see color? Deer have *dichromatic* color vision, meaning they probably see colors as do humans with color blindness. As a result, the various shades of brown, green, yellow, orange and red tend to be seen as yellow.

Humans know that as light fades to dark, it becomes more difficult to distinguish colors. Since deer are very active in low-light conditions, and since they have the ability to see in the ultraviolet spectrum, this probably means that seeing color is not as important for deer as for humans. We do know that deer have many more *rods* (which are black and white receptors) than *cones* (color receptors). However, it is most likely that the deer's scattered cones allow them to see or distinguish between a few colors.

Testing to determine if deer can see color is very difficult. This is because deer might use brightness to discriminate rather than the actual color. However, some tests indicate that close relatives of the deer can see some form of color. One study showed that elk could tell orange from other colors (however, brightness may have affected those results). Other studies show that red deer can distinguish various colors. The speculation is that the more light, the more perception deer have of certain colors. Less light gives less perception of color. Several researchers suggest that even though deer can distinguish between a few colors, they may not need that ability to survive in the wild.

Choosing Camouflage Patterns

So what's the value of wearing camouflage hunting clothes if whitetails don't see colors the same as you do? The answer may lie in the deer's ability to distinguish brightness.

Studies have shown that deer can assess brightness, although not as well as humans. What this means to hunters is that a camouflage pattern that uses large areas of dark and light colors for maximum contrast will best break up the human outline. Camouflage clothes with too "fine" a pattern appear to be a solid color when viewed from a distance. As a result, they lack contrast in brightness and are more easily seen by deer.

During open firearms seasons, hunters are often required to wear blaze-orange clothing for safety reasons. Where legal, hunters choosing a blaze-orange camouflage pattern are easily seen by other hunters, yet probably are as invisible to deer as they would be in their favorite brown, gray, green or white patterns.

Of course, the most important factor to avoid being spotted by deer is to remain motionless. While it is impossible never to move, you can hide much of your movement by leaving as much natural cover around you as possible.

CHOOSE the proper camouflage pattern to fool the whitetail's eyesight from opening day (top), through mid-fall (left) and the open firearms season (middle), until the close of the late season (right).

Whitetail Populations
& Habitats

Populations

Whitetail populations in the United States and Canada have always been strongly tied to habitat quality; the better the habitat, the greater the deer numbers. Historically, the quality of that wildlife habitat has been determined largely by how humans choose to use the land.

In precolonial times, tens of millions of whitetails roamed the forests of North America, vastly outnumbering the Indians who hunted them. But by the early 1900s, the whitetail population had fallen drastically as European immigrants flowed into North America, bringing extensive agricultural and industrial development with them.

An equally dramatic shift occurred between 1950 and the 1990s, as whitetails rebounded to a stable population, now estimated at over 20 million. The reasons for this dramatic resurgence are as simple as they are remarkable. Over the past 50 years, we have recognized the dangers that human activities pose to deer and other wildlife, and we've found the means and determination to protect the needs of those species.

Whitetail Numbers, Past and Present

Through evidence found at archaeological digs, anthropologists know that whitetail deer have been an important source of food, tools and clothing for American Indians since the last ice age. The abundance of whitetail remains in these sites suggests that the whitetail has been one of the continent's most common big game animals for a very long time. It is likely that the overall whitetail population numbered between 24 and 33 million during precolonial times. In most of North America, there were probably 8 to 10 deer per square mile, but concentrations of 20 to 30 deer per square mile probably existed in some areas.

Indians traded deer hides with Europeans for knives, clothing and other supplies. Some experts estimate that they harvested 4½ to 6½ million whitetails each year to satisfy this booming fur trade. As a result, the continent's deer herd was reduced to approximately 10 to 15 million by the year 1800.

In the early 1800s, settlers began to displace Indians on the west side of the Appalachians. During this transition, whitetails gained a few years of protection from market demand. At about the same time, they probably expanded into new habitats and returned to parts of the East where they had earlier been eliminated. This

temporary relief may have allowed the continent's whitetail population to recover slightly.

But beginning in about 1850 and lasting until 1900, whitetail numbers started on a downward spiral and eventually reached a record low of only a few hundred thousand. In fact, deer were eliminated completely in parts of the East and Midwest. Massive harvests by market hunters and subsistence hunting by settlers played a pivotal role in this collapse, but habitat loss, though more subtle, was probably just as lethal.

Hunters and their 3-day harvest of whitetails taken near Phillips, Wisconsin, in 1880

During the last half of the nineteenth century, the North American landscape was transformed. When settlers pushed westward, more and more land was used for farming and industry, and whitetail habitat melted away.

In the late 1800s and early 1900s, massive logging operations denuded millions of acres of forest. The state of New York was completely forested in pre-colonial times, but by 1880 more than 75 percent of the land had been logged and cleared. Much of the land clear-cut during this period served as grazing

land for sheep and cattle or was plowed under for row crops and small grains. These activities destroyed much prime whitetail habitat.

Beginning in the 1930s, deer numbers started to rebound due to new laws that ended market hunting, set restrictive hunting seasons and protected whitetail does from hunters. The Pittman-Robertson Act of 1937 collected excise taxes on arms and ammunition, then distributed the money to state wildlife agencies for wildlife research and habitat management. Whitetails were among the first game animals to benefit

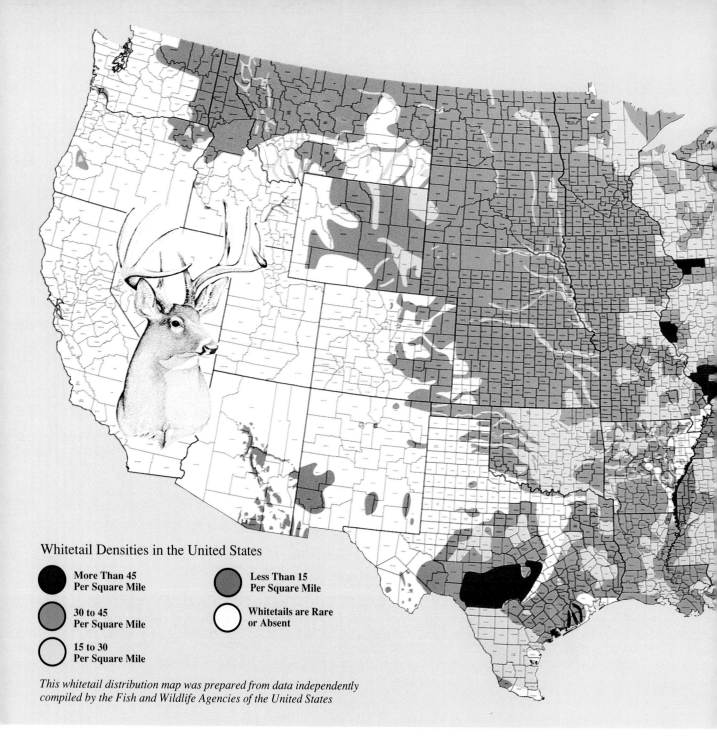

Whitetail Densities in the United States

- ● More Than 45 Per Square Mile
- ● 30 to 45 Per Square Mile
- ○ 15 to 30 Per Square Mile
- ◐ Less Than 15 Per Square Mile
- ○ Whitetails are Rare or Absent

This whitetail distribution map was prepared from data independently compiled by the Fish and Wildlife Agencies of the United States

from this new era of well-financed, scientific wildlife management. Conservationists in many of the northeastern states had worried about the extinction of whitetails at the turn of the century – by the late 1930s, they watched deer numbers soar to maximums of 50 to 80 animals per square mile in some areas.

By the 1960s, efforts to control harvests and improve whitetail habitat were showing clear results, with whitetail herds growing rapidly almost everywhere. "Bucks-only" harvest strategies encouraged the species to reach its reproductive potential. Successful fire-prevention efforts allowed woody vegetation to move into grasslands, and limited timber harvests

created additional areas of brushy growth that offered food and cover for deer.

Whitetail numbers increased dramatically across the species' range through the 1970s and 1980s, peaking in the early 1990s. Populations reached historic highs in eastern hardwoods, midwestern farm country, western river bottoms, and throughout the South and Southeast. In areas that once held 10 to 15 deer per square mile, it was now common to find as many as 30 deer per square mile.

Improvements in habitat and successful regulation of hunting have brought deer numbers to modern-day

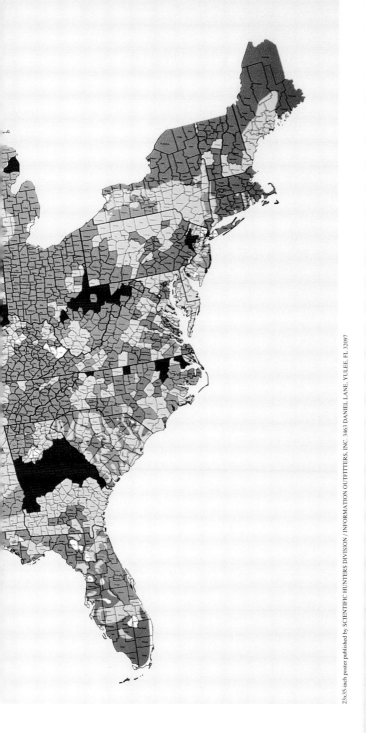

23x35-inch poster published by SCIENTIFIC HUNTERS DIVISION / INFORMATION OUTFITTERS, INC. 3463 DANIEL LANE, YULEE, FL 32097

Too Many Deer

When suburban deer populations get too high, there is an increased incidence of Lyme disease transmitted to humans from deer ticks, auto/deer collisions become an everyday occurance, and backyard gardens and shrubs are severely damaged by browsing whitetails. The most commonly used, safest, and most economical solution to deer overpopulation is a controlled bowhunt. However, this solution usually elicits strong objections from animal rights believers in the area. They often suggest that a deer contraception program be initiated. There are several reasons why contraception is not practical.

First, several federal and state agencies control the use of drugs like the ones that would be used in deer contraception. Getting the permits to use these drugs can be a drawn-out process requiring research on the effects these drugs may have on the environment. Few states have sought these permits or launched this kind of research.

Second, a chemical compound needs to be developed that can sterilize does with just one injection. That also has not been developed to date.

Third, the effects of such a chemical compound on deer behavior need to be studied. If a doe does not get pregnant, she may remain in estrus throughout the winter. Thus, bucks would actively pursue such does at a time when they normally would be striving to conserve energy. This could have devastating effects on survival, effects that might be difficult to foresee or control.

Fourth, deer contraception is almost impossible to administer to all the breeding females. For example, if deer managers locate 75 percent of the breeding does in a population, treat 80 percent of them and the contraceptive has a 90 percent efficacy, then 46 percent of the does *still* remain reproductively active.

Finally, attempting a contraceptive program is costly. Research shows that to stabilize a deer herd, the cost is $533 per doe treated. If you needed to treat 200 does, then the cost would be approximately $106,600. Few towns can afford such costs, especially when a bowhunt can be conducted at virtually no cost to the community.

Animal rights leaders also suggest introducing predators to control deer numbers, but bringing wolves, coyotes or mountain lions into suburban areas is impossible and impractical. Likewise, the suggestion to "let nature take care of her own" might have worked 200 years ago, but today it will lead to suffering of deer, habitat destruction and widespread damage to private property. Another option, trapping and transplanting deer, also has been shown to be ineffective, because deer introduced into new habitats die within 6 months of the move.

The conclusion is that harvesting some deer is the only proven method of lessening suburban deer problems. Though this approach may not please 100 percent of the citizenry, it does appeal to the large majority.

highs in much of North America. Hunters have benefited, of course, since wildlife management agencies have begun to institute more liberal bag limits in an effort to control growing deer populations. In areas of New Jersey and West Virginia, for example, where deer densities have occasionally reached 80 animals per square mile, the legal harvest can be as high as 30 deer per square mile. But other groups – farmers, for example – view the large deer population as an economic liability.

The challenge to state wildlife agencies is to manage deer at levels that satisfy all concerns – a difficult job, but one our wildlife professionals have done admirably.

Habitats

From wetlands to deserts, deep woods to farm fields, whitetails adapt and survive, but they thrive only where habitat, food and cover are optimum. The better the habitat, the larger the whitetail population and the healthier each individual deer. Whitetails do well in forests where there is plenty of browse and in agriculture areas where forage is unusually rich and abundant.

Quality habitats start with soil fertility and moisture. Deep, rich soils and abundant rains combine to grow varied and dense vegetation, creating a cornucopia of forage and unlimited hiding places. In farm country, wood lots, wetlands, streamside thickets and hedgerows provide escape cover, while fertilized crops supply superior nutrition. Timber cutting in native forests opens soils to sunlight. which fuels vigorous vegetative growth rich in protein and minerals. In the North, dense conifer forests create excellent shelter, but often low-quality forage. Lichens growing on lower tree branches become available and important as snow deepens in traditional deer yards. In the West, irrigated croplands often fuel an explosion in local whitetail populations that have been living in the rather limited woody habitat along rivers and creeks. Not surprisingly, deer do well on rich, fertile, glaciated soils in the northern United States, especially in conjunction with croplands. Let's consider some of the most important whitetail habitats, beginning in the West.

Deer wintering beneath mature conifers

NORTHERN ROCKY MOUNTAINS. This area covers mountains, rolling hills, plateaus and river valleys from eastern Washington through northern Idaho, Montana, and central and eastern Wyoming. Whitetails in this region live wherever they find suitable habitat from 900 feet above sea level in valleys to 6,500 feet up mountain slopes. Major habitats include cottonwood and willow communities along rivers and mixed conifer/shrub communities at higher elevations. Portions of this region are heavily farmed. These fertilized, irrigated croplands provide critical winter forage, which enables populations to reach unusually high densities for the region. Whitetails are native in the northern Rockies, but populations were historically low. They increased to high levels in portions of the range in the 1940s, but, thereafter, habitat losses led to a major decline. Today, populations are again high, and whitetails are spreading along major rivers. Small burns and clear-cuts (20 acres or less) in forests provide forage.

SOUTHERN ROCKY MOUNTAINS. Texas and Coues' deer are the two subspecies living in localized pockets of hilly to mountainous habitat in southeastern Arizona and southwestern New Mexico. This is rough country with steep canyons. Vegetation includes coniferous forests and oak woodlands. Riparian areas (habitat adjacent to streams and rivers) and desert grasslands are important because annual rainfall is only 10 to 20 inches. Apparently the Coues' deer was more abundant in the late 1800s than it is today. As domestic livestock increased and riparian habitat was lost, numbers of deer diminished. Human demand for water has driven the water table down and dried up many perennial streams and springs – critical factors. In addition, the reproductive potential of Coues' deer is less than that of other whitetails. Only 75 percent of 2-year-olds give birth, and then, to usually just one fawn. Coues' deer eat many plant species, but mountain mahogany is most important. Droughts and habitat loss are the two major limiting factors.

PLAINS. This large, diverse area runs from south central Canada south through Montana and North Dakota to New Mexico and northwestern Texas. Most of this region is grassland and farm fields, so whitetails concentrate along draws, swales, sloughs, river floodplains and stream bottoms. Tree growth is primarily found only along rivers and streams and in man-made wood lots and shelterbelts. Major species include ash, elm, aspen and juniper to the north; cottonwood and oaks to the south. In much

MIDWEST. This vast region stretches from south central Canada south to Oklahoma and from central Nebraska east to Kentucky. Major habitats include mixed aspen and conifer forests in the north, agriculture lands in the central United States and oak/hickory forests in the south. The combination of deciduous forests along stream bottoms, interspersed with thick cover from abandoned farmed areas, plus good food provided by agriculture croplands creates large-bodied, older whitetails with exceptionally large antlers. Winters would not normally kill deer in the Midwest, but when there is an acorn crop failure combined with a harsh winter, deer mortality can occur in localized areas.

of the central and southern plains, standing cornfields provide deer with large expanses of cover during summer and early fall. These fields allow whitetails to disperse far from traditional cover. In the northern and central plains where deep snow covers crops, deer are forced to search for browse in shelterbelts and forested river bottoms.

NORTHEAST. This area reaches from southeastern Canada and Maine south through New York and into northern Pennsylvania and New Jersey. Forests consist primarily of beech, birch, maple, spruce and fir trees. Most of the area is laced with rivers, lakes and bogs. In northern and mountainous parts of the region, deep snow and periods of extended cold force deer to concentrate around coniferous trees, which catch much of the snow.

APPALACHIAN MOUNTAINS. This heavily forested region extends from Pennsylvania and Ohio south to Alabama. Major tree types are black cherry, hemlock, birch, ash and maple to the north; oak, poplar, pine and hickory to the south. Portions of these mountains have low soil fertility and thus, low-quality forage for deer. Deep snow and severe cold limit deer numbers in the northern Appalachian Mountains.

PIEDMONT PLATEAU. Bordering the eastern edge of the Appalachian Mountains from Maryland south to Alabama, much of this area is forested with oak and hickory in the north and mixed pine and hardwoods in the south. Numerous streams wind through the hilly landscape. Since timber is economically important here, the manner in which it is harvested greatly affects local deer herds.

COASTAL PLAIN. This area extends along the Atlantic and Gulf coasts from New York through southern Texas, and up the Mississippi River to Missouri and southern Illinois. Much of the coastal plain consists of marshes, plains, sandy beaches and swamps. Half of the coastal plain is farmed, with two-thirds in pasture and one-third in cultivated crops such as soybeans, corn, cotton, rice and peanuts. Forested lands consist of various pine species, oak, cypress, juniper, hickory, willow and cottonwood. In the past, forests in this region were managed solely for timber, but today, foresters commonly leave hardwood stands in river bottoms and have tailored the size and shape of clear-cuts to favor deer and other wildlife. Throughout the region, hot, humid weather contributes to a high incidence of diseases and parasites in whitetails, but it also produces abundant forage.

TEXAS. Due to its large size, this state has a wide variety of habitats, from mountainous areas in the west to coastal plains in southern and eastern Texas. Deer densities also vary greatly. In fact, in many parts of the state, whitetails are rare or totally absent, while other pockets have over 65 deer per square mile.

The two most-recognized whitetail regions in Texas are the South Texas Plains (above) and the Edwards Plateau (inset above) in west central Texas. The latter, often called the "Hill Country," is known for its high deer densities, averaging about 40 deer per square mile. About one-half of the state's whitetails live in this region. The Edwards Plateau is primarily rangeland covered with bluestem and switchgrass, heavily grazed by both cattle and deer. Predominant cover types in the region include mesquite and a variety of oaks.

The South Texas Plains, also known as the "Brush Country," owes its exceptional whitetail hunting to the excellent management practices applied by its landowners. Bucks living on large, privately owned ranches are often protected until they reach their full trophy potential. Whitetail deer densities are moderate throughout much of the region, which leaves an abundance of forage. Much of the South Texas Plains is covered by a dense canopy of mesquite, prickly pear, whitebrush and a variety of oaks and acacias, a thorny, shrublike tree with clusters of white and yellow flowers.

Droughts have a major impact on deer numbers in much of Texas. In addition, predators, especially coyotes, are responsible for heavy fawn losses in various areas, and studies indicate that they can actually limit deer numbers in portions of southern and eastern Texas.

Foods & Feeding

and finishes chewing. Then the many microorganisms and complex chemical reactions in the stomach go to work, digesting plant material and supplying the deer with energy.

Deer are *ruminants*. That means they have four-chambered stomachs that use an extensive array of symbiotic bacteria, protozoans, acid and enzymes to digest foods. The first chamber in the stomach, called the *rumen,* stores partially chewed food and allows a deer to feed quickly as the opportunity presents itself. Later, when the deer is safely bedded in heavy cover, it regurgitates the *bolus* or *cud* of food

Deer feed nearly everywhere, and they consume hundreds of plant species. This gives the impression that they are not selective eaters. This definitely is not true. When it comes to groceries, deer are picky. Since they are small compared to ruminants like elk and moose, they prefer foods that yield a lot of energy and don't take too long to digest. This is typically new plant growth with relatively low concentrations of "roughage" like cellulose and lignin. When a deer has a choice, it will nip the growing ends off the plants it eats, since these rapidly growing tissues contain more protein and nitrogen than the older growth lower on the plant.

Whitetails consume many foods, including grasses, tree leaves (both green and dead), mast (especially acorns, but also nuts of many other woody plants), mushrooms and the green leaves and twigs of various woody plants. Among the most nutritious deer foods are green, succulent vegetation; both soft and hard mast (especially acorns); fruits of hawthorn, grape, persimmon, sumac and greenbrier; and mushrooms.

Some of these foods appear and disappear with the seasons. Acorns are a prime food that disappears quickly as squirrels and other small mammals hoard them in the fall. Corn, soybeans, alfalfa, apples and other crops are also superb forage, but they disappear with harvest or the end of the growing season. Many deer foods are buried out of reach after heavy snow.

And sometimes food is scarce because deer have eaten it all. In areas with too many deer, many preferred foods are limited because of over-browsing. In these situations, deer consume large amounts of woody browse. Though not as nutritious as other kinds of whitetail food, woody browse does have one advantage – it is often abundant in deer habitat, especially where commercial timbering is common. The slash left in the wake of timber cutting brings plenty of green forage down to the deer's level.

If deer run out of menu options, they finally resort to "filler food." These plants provide very little nutrition but will fill a deer's stomach. The winter diets of northern whitetails may include a number of these fillers, including species such as rhododendron, hemlock, aspen and pine.

DIGESTION in deer is similar to that of cattle and sheep; they quickly consume forage, store it in the (1) *rumen* (the largest part of the stomach), regurgitate it to chew their *cud*, and then digest it. This process allows deer to minimize the time they spend feeding in open areas and to return to the safety of heavy cover. Once food is regurgitated, chewed and swallowed again, microorganisms in the rumen begin to digest the cellulose. The food is then moved to the (2) *reticulum*, the second chamber of the stomach, where it ferments. From here, the partially digested fiber moves to the (3) *omasum* and the (4) *abomasum,* where complete digestion occurs.

THE INTESTINAL TRACT of a pregnant or nursing doe is longer than that of a buck due to her higher nutrient requirements. Thus, a doe with fawns probably selects habitats with the best possible foods to gain the needed nutrients. In general, bucks use forest habitats while does prefer open grasslands with more and improved forage.

Seasonal Foods

In early spring (March to May), deer forage on herbaceous plants, with some browsing of woody plants. In late spring (May to June), about half a deer's diet is green leaves, but large quantities of agricultural crops are also consumed. In summer, deer eat agricultural crops and new woody tree twigs and stems. In fall, deer eat a variety of crops, woody browse and green leaves. However, they also pick up acorns, beechnuts and other mast, and fruits that fall to the ground.

Deer typically lose weight over winter, even when they have good forage. The key to a whitetail's survival during the winter is how fast it loses weight. The rate of weight loss depends on how much forage is available, how much nutritional value it has and how much energy the deer has to spend to get it. In much of the whitetail's range, snow covers most foods at ground level. If the snow isn't too deep, deer will dig down for acorns, waste corn and grass. In these conditions, a surprisingly high percentage of their winter diet can be dead leaves. As snow deepens, however, the forage offered by shrubs and trees standing above the snow becomes increasingly important. Whitetails in the northeastern United States feed on greenbrier because it is high in protein, stands above heavy snows during the worst winters and can withstand heavy browsing. Deer in this region also browse on blackberry, maple, sumac and many other woody species.

Deer are opportunistic feeders, eating what is available; but if we had to ignore regional differences in the whitetail menu and name the ONE most preferred deer food, it would be oak acorns. Where they are available, acorns are readily consumed in fall and will also be eaten in winter as long as snow isn't too deep (see graph below). During years with heavy acorn crops, acorns are a mainstay until summer, when they are no longer available.

Red oak leaf (left) and white oak leaf (right)

Whitetails prefer white oak acorns, probably because they contain less of the bitter chemical, tannin, than acorns from members of the red oak group. A hunter shouldn't have too much trouble recognizing trees of the white oak group – white oak leaves have round lobes, while those of the more common red oak are pointed (above).

Agricultural crops are also important foods in most whitetail habitats. The crops most preferred include alfalfa, soybeans, sugar beets, corn, beans, peas, sweet potatoes, wheat and apples.

Regional Foods

As whitetail habitat varies considerably across North America, so too does the whitetail's diet. Oddly enough, deer in some regions will eat a given plant while deer in other regions will have nothing to do with it. Deer in northern West Virginia don't care for sassafras leaves; for deer in central Pennsylvania, sassafras is a staple. Deer in parts of Missouri and Michigan prefer red cedar, but deer in the Southeast don't eat it. And red maple twigs are browsed heavily in northern ranges but much less in the Southeast. Nobody knows for sure why such differences exist, but they are probably related to variations in the chemical composition of the plants, which may in turn be related to differences in soils. Let's look at some of the more important foods for deer living in various habitats, starting with the Northwest.

Acorn Consumption in Whitetails

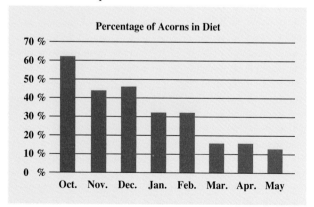

THE STOMACH CONTENTS of 440 whitetails were examined over an 8-month period by Missouri biologists. The results (above) indicate that acorns, when available, are an important food for deer from fall through spring.

NORTHERN ROCKY MOUNTAINS. Whitetails in this region prefer agricultural crops, especially alfalfa, sugar beets and winter wheat. Deer eat woody plants, especially aspen and cottonwoods, and evergreens, especially Douglas fir and western red cedar. Deer also consume Saskatoon serviceberry, snowberry, creeping mahonia and redstem ceanothus.

SOUTHERN ROCKY MOUNTAINS. Whitetails in this high mountain and desert basin landscape eat a variety of woody browse and forbs. Perhaps the most important browse species is mountain mahogany. Deer in this region also scarf down desert ceanothus, skunkbush sumac, silktassel, filaree, vetch, fleabane, false tarragon, sagebrush and coralbells.

PLAINS. Important foods for deer in the northern plains include sumac, dogwood, serviceberry, choke-berry, greasewood, bearberry, rose, sagebrush and Douglas fir. To the south, deer eat alfalfa, corn, wheat, sunflower, various oaks, cottonwood, snowberry and many types of grasses.

MIDWEST. In the northern Midwest, white cedar and beaked hazel are important browse species. Cedar boughs can sustain deer during long northern winters. One northern Minnesota study showed beaked hazel to be the number one winter food for deer. It is especially abundant and important in the upper Great Lakes region. Winter foods in the north also include mountain ash, white cedar, red maple and hemlock. In the oak/hickory forests farther south, the major diet item is acorns. Deer in this region also eat grape, sumac, honeysuckle, dogwood, serviceberry and greenbrier. When available, corn, soybeans, sorghum and winter wheat are important foods. Obviously, in the agricultural area of the Midwest, the major diet items are crops, including corn, soybeans and other grains. Fields close to thick cover, river bottoms or water are preferred. In late fall, deer may even bed in unharvested corn.

NORTHEAST. As in all areas with oak timber, the number-one diet item for northeastern whitetails is acorns, but they also consume white cedar, hemlock, mountain ash, red maple, mountain laurel, various fruits, witch hobble, dead and live tree leaves and broadleaf herbaceous plants. Deer in the northern-most habitats in this region often eat lichens in the fall and winter, especially those growing on the trunks and lower branches of trees. During heavy snows, deer gravitate toward dense conifer cover where lichens are more abundant.

APPALACHIAN MOUNTAINS. Diets of whitetails in the Appalachians are similar to those of deer in the Northeast, but additional preferred items include greenbrier, grape, red cedar, sumac, blackberry, hon-eysuckle and persimmon. Deer in this region also

Buck searching for food buried by snow

graze on acorns, dead leaves, crops, clovers and various grasses.

PIEDMONT PLATEAU. Japanese honeysuckle is a favorite year-round food for deer living in the Piedmont Plateau. They also consume large quantities of acorns whenever available, in addition to privet, green leaves of hardwood species and fruits of greenbrier, sumac and grape.

COASTAL PLAIN. Whitetail diets in this region vary tremendously – acorns, beautyberry, trumpet creeper, hawthorns, persimmon, holly, mulberry, black gum, blackberry, greenbrier and grape are staples – but dozens of other plants also turn up in the coastal whitetail's menu.

TEXAS. Acorns are a staple food for deer in Texas oak country, but deer also consume large quantities of forbs and grasses. Oak leaves and woody browse are important, as are sedges. Staple food species include blackberry, persimmon, honey mesquite and cacti. In the important South Texas Plains, prickly pears are important in the diet.

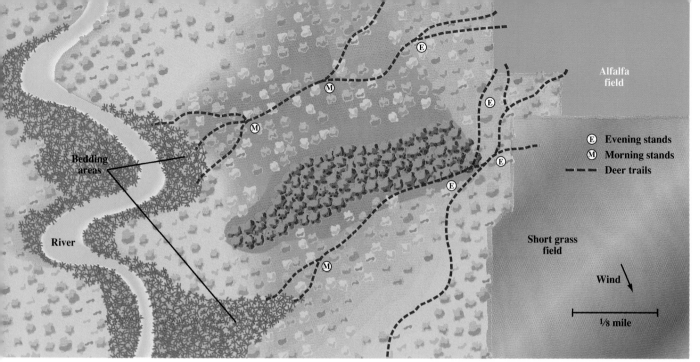

AMBUSH whitetails as they move between bedding and feeding areas by using well-placed stands. Morning stands should be close to the bedding areas, but not so close that you disturb deer when you exit the stand. Place evening stands near feed fields, but far enough back in the woods that deer pass through during good shooting light.

Feeding Patterns

Deer like stream valleys, not only because there is a dependable supply of water but because bottom lands provide good cover and exceptional forage. Researchers speculate that creek bottom soils are unusually rich, thus producing nutritious forage plants. Such areas are especially important during dry summers. Early fall will also find deer using stream valleys.

Deer also feed in areas where timbering and fire have set back plant succession. Timbering allows more light to reach the forest floor, stimulating growth of the succulent vegetation deer prefer. Fire has the same effect.

Deer wander through a feeding area, stopping to nip foods that smell and taste good. If there is plenty of food, they will remain in that area, sometimes for many hours. If foods are sparse, deer feed little and move rapidly, searching for more productive areas.

Since most deer are seen at dawn and dusk, casual observers assume that most of their feeding is done at these times. This is not true, because most deer feed predominately after dark. Although deer are active in the morning and evening (going to and from feeding and bedding areas) they feed little at this time. Deer have small peaks of feeding activity beginning around noon and larger peaks just before dusk, but most feeding is done after dark.

Dr. Harry Jacobson, deer biologist at Mississippi State University, used automatic cameras at artificial feeding stations to determine when deer feed. After examining 14,501 photos, he found that feeding activity was mostly after dark, year-round. Major periods began at 6:00 P.M. (dusk) through 9:00 P.M. Activity continued all night, with secondary peaks at 11:00 P.M. and 5:00 A.M. Hunters should note that deer fed after sunrise more often in the fall than in other seasons of the year.

In the northern parts of deer range, cold temperatures force deer to congregate in sheltered areas. These are often called "deer yards." The amount of time northern deer spend in yards depends on the severity of the winter. The packed trails in deer yards help deer conserve energy, and they may help them escape wolves as well. Northern white cedar is the most important plant species in deer yards, providing both food and cover.

Deep snow can trap deer in areas with limited food supply. If the snow persists, many deer may starve, but deer can fast for several weeks in winter, so only extended cold and deep snows pose a serious problem. Well-meaning citizens often begin feeding programs to help deer survive. These efforts seldom succeed. In order to digest hay or other domestic forage, deer need to change the bacteria in their stomachs. Since this shift takes weeks to occur, deer may die with stomachs full of food they were unable to digest. And, even when administered gradually, supplemental feeding may concentrate deer and increase disease and predation.

Deer habitat can be improved by logging

Improving Foods for Whitetails

Timbering can lead to rapid growth of new vegetation and improve habitat for deer. However there are many factors that affect the regeneration of plants in a recently timbered area. The quality of the soil, the amount of sunlight, the presence or absence of nearby seed sources for new vegetation and competition among plants all help determine the kinds of plants and the density of plant growth that invade a cut. Numbers of deer in the area may also have an effect, since heavy browsing can eliminate preferred forage plants before they fully establish themselves. If timbering leads to rapid growth of tree seedlings, they may outgrow the reach of deer within 2 to 3 years. If you're planning to cut a piece of timber, you might want to consider contacting a forester and wildlife biologist to make sure cutting can be done to provide more food for deer.

Timber operations in the Southeast plant huge tracts of loblolly pine because it grows fast and commands a good price. With the right management, loblolly pine plantations can sustain reasonable whitetail populations. The key is thinning the stand. Repeated light thinning of loblolly pine at 20, 25, and 30 years yields more ground vegetation than a single heavy cutting.

On rich soils, light thinning of oaks is the best way to encourage desirable deer foods, but heavy thinning is needed on poorer quality sites. Leaving selected crop trees and cutting everything else on lower mountain slopes gives greater browse production than does similar cutting on higher slopes.

Deer biologists in the Northeast have recommended thinning regimes for several popular kinds of timber. In white pine stands, they suggest doing the first thinning when the trees are about 40 years old. For hemlock plantations, the biologists recommend that the stand be thinned at the same time regeneration cuts are made. In spruce-fir timber, the experts recommend that the stand be thinned before it is 30 years old.

Because acorns are so important to deer in hardwood forests, management of oaks is a key part of effective deer management. Most oaks reach maximum acorn production at 40 years of age – the rotation of cutting should be planned with that fact in mind. It's a good idea to encourage a variety of oak species, too. Most of the red oak group takes two years to produce a crop of acorns, while the white oaks produce their acorns in a single year. A mix of species from the two groups will minimize the chance of a complete acorn crop failure after a killing frost. A variety of species helps minimize the impact of oak diseases, too. Oak stands should be thinned periodically, but leave the best of the mature trees to enhance acorn production. Nothing is more important for whitetails than mature oak stands. A careful manager can derive a good income from his oaks and produce excellent crops of acorns and whitetails at the same time.

Clear-cuts can provide great feeding habitat for deer, but the size of cuts is important. Though large cuts lead to much vegetative growth, within a few short years the foods have grown beyond the reach of deer. Such areas

Texas bucks feeding on deer pellets

develop heavy canopy cover, which reduces under-growth for many years to come. If deer production is a priority in your timber, it's best to limit the size of cuts to 5 to 10 acres. Plan for a 20-year difference in age between adjacent cuts, and make your cuts long, with irregular edges, rather than square.

Fire in logged areas reduces debris, improves seed-bed and stimulates growth of desirable deer forage. Natural fires once kept forests more open, providing deer food at ground level. Today, controlled burning is recognized as a valuable tool for managing deer habitat (right). In southern pine stands, a spring burn every 3 to 5 years benefits deer. However, it's not a good idea to burn oak stands – even a cool ground fire may injure oak trees and impair subsequent acorn production. Timber managers in the South and parts of the West commonly use controlled burns to improve the commercial value of a forest, but fire is seldom used as a timber management tool in the Northeast. Many residents still remember the notori-ous wild fires that once scarred many parts of the region. Without regular fires, the Northeast's forests continue to accumulate dry downed timber. This growing stockpile of potential fuel makes controlled burning difficult and increases the risk of another wild fire as well.

Controlled burn

Supplemental Feeding

There are three forms of supplemental food programs that benefit deer: they are food plots, mineral supplements and food supplements. Game management agencies and hunting clubs have maintained food plots for many years. These plots are still being used, but today there is renewed interest in the use of supplemental foods and minerals. Supplemental feeding is not a "quick fix" for good deer habitat. However, it can improve deer growth and health and provide missing nutrients during certain seasons.

Food plots for deer provide cover and digestible, nutritious vegetation to supplement natural forage. Plant selection varies with climate, soil and local growing conditions. The species chosen should be easy and cost-effective to establish. Examples are: switchgrass, clovers, soybeans, corn, alfalfa, winter wheat, perennial rye grasses and apple trees. In the North, managers often start small patches of alfalfa, clovers or corn in clear-cuts to provide high-protein year-round supplemental food. Soybeans are also high in protein but are only available in the summer and fall. Cereal grains mixed with legumes are commonly used for whitetail food plots in the Midwest and South.

County extension agents can assist you in selecting appropriate species. Establishing a food plot will cost from $50 to $100 per acre. Clover is a staple for most whitetails, and it works well in food plots in most parts of the country. Plant clover when weather is cool and wet, typically spring and fall in the North, winter in the South. Time fall plantings 2 months before a heavy freeze.

Deer don't need salt blocks, but they will use them. Calcium and phosphorus mineral blocks can contribute to better antler production, especially in mineral-deficient soils. Granular minerals in troughs are even better because they can be mixed with supplemental feed and troughs can be cleaned to reduce the risk of disease.

Supplemental food has been used a great deal in Texas and other regions of the South. Corn is probably the most commonly used supplemental food for deer. Various pelleted foods are also used (opposite page). Corn is high in carbohydrates, low in protein and makes a good late fall and winter food. In midwinter, mix two parts corn with one part protein pellets. At winter's end, raise the amount of protein pellets you're offering as deer begin to grow antlers and reproduce.

The Question of Baiting. . .

Hunting deer over piles of bait such as sugar beets, corn, apples and carrots is illegal in most states but legal in some. In Michigan, baiting is commonly used to harvest deer, and the sale of hundreds of tons of sugar beets and carrots at rural stores has become a multimillion-dollar industry. Baiting is most effective when normal food supplies are limited. For example, when deep snow covers forage in the Midwest, deer will travel by the dozens to a well-stocked bait site.

But baiting can also cause several problems. Some of these bait sites are unsightly and offensive. If one owner baits and another does not, deer concentrate around the bait. This may lead to "defensive baiting," where a landowner has no choice but to join in the baiting battle if he hopes to have any deer on his property.

Where baiting deer is legal, the question of whether it is ethical is being asked by more and more hunters. Many feel that taking an animal over a bait pile is not "fair chase," and as a result, wrong. However, this question is complex. Animal rightists could carry it to extremes by suggesting that hunting near cornfields or acorns is "baiting," and therefore should be illegal. Interestingly, few people in Texas or Saskatchewan are opposed to the use of corn and other baits, while the practice of using sugar beets and carrots is hotly debated in Michigan.

Baiting is not a biological problem, but it does raise sociological issues that will be argued over for years to come. This is especially true in urban areas where hunting is not as much of a tradition as it is in rural communities.

Communication

Whitetails communicate both visually and vocally through a complex interplay of body language and calls. The hunter who learns this language can use it to distinct advantage.

Vocalizations

Vocal calls are important to whitetails because they spend much time in thick cover where visual signals are difficult or impossible to see. Not counting a *foot-stomp* used to express mild alarm (opposite page), deer employ about a dozen different calls. From the hunter's view, whitetail vocalizations can be divided into three categories.

DOE-FAWN CALLS. A doe typically beds her fawn during the day when she leaves to feed, then announces her return with a *maternal grunt*. This begins quietly, but increases in volume if the doe does not soon hear a reply. The fawn responds with a delicate, barely audible *mew* call, which begins at a medium pitch, then descends. Humans can easily imitate the sound by mouth. Once the doe and fawn are reunited, the hungry youngster makes a *nursing whine* as it begins to suckle. This call probably helps the doe identify the fawn and also strengthens the maternal bond.

When separated from its mother, a fawn *bleats* much like a lamb. It will *bawl* loudly when distressed or frightened. Research shows that most females recognize the bawls made by their own young. Doe-fawn calls are seldom useful to hunters, although a fawn bleat or bawl can sometimes lure a doe into view.

ALARM CALLS. Adult whitetails indicate varying levels of alarm with several calls. A deer that is moderately alarmed *snorts* a sharp blast of air through its nostrils. This is the sound most hunters hear just before a deer bounds away. Deer often snort repeatedly when they sense possible danger but have not confirmed it or do not yet feel directly threatened. When a deer is extremely frightened or in the grip of a predator, it may *bawl* repeatedly. This alarm bawl is an intense, loud, low-pitched, chilling cry that

resembles the commercial injured-rabbit calls hunters often use to attract predators.

Yearling deer are more likely to bawl than are experienced adult deer. Like doe-fawn calls, alarm calls are rarely mimicked by hunters, since these are likely to alert deer to danger. But an alarm call can rouse a hidden deer from its bed or shock an escaping deer into stopping briefly.

BREEDING CALLS. During mating season, bucks become quite vocal by deer standards, both with does and with competing bucks. Most commercial deer calls are designed to mimic these sounds, and a hunter who learns to use them greatly increases his chances for success.

Deer employ several distinct grunt calls during aggressive dominance displays. A dominant deer of either sex may give a *low grunt*. This is a single, abrupt call that sounds much like a burp. It's low in pitch and volume and audible only at close range. The low grunt is often heard in the early phases of a sparring match between bucks. The *grunt-snort* indicates that hostilities between two deer have increased. This intense "huhh, huhh, huhh, huhh" sound results from a deer forcing air through its nostrils in a series of three to six brief blasts, spaced 1 to 2 seconds apart. A doe may sometimes grunt-snort, but normally this is a buck challenge call usually preceded by a low grunt.

As a dominance confrontation between two mature bucks escalates, the grunt-snort may change into a *grunt-snort wheeze*. This begins with a series of grunt-snorts followed immediately by a drawn-out wheeze that sounds like compressed air hissing from a punctured tire.

Most hunters have heard the familiar *tending grunt* of a buck scent-trailing a doe in heat or courting her. Longer in duration than the low grunt, the tending grunt consists of three or more "urrp, urrp, urrp" sounds repeated at 2- to 3-second intervals. Volume and intensity vary depending on the situation.

The tending grunt is perhaps the most important call for hunters. Because it indicates a buck has found a

Alert buck foot-stomping

doe in estrus, a well-executed tending grunt will often attract other bucks. It is not, however, a sure-fire strategy. A buck may respond to a grunt call eagerly one day and ignore it the next, perhaps because he was recently defeated by a dominant animal. Given another 2 or 3 days, the buck might regain his confidence and again respond aggressively to an imitation grunt.

Most hunters call too often and too emphatically. Once a deer is moving your way, don't call again unless he stops or moves away. Remember that white-tails have remarkably sensitive hearing; humans often call at a volume that seems unnaturally loud to deer. The very best way to learn to mimic whitetail vocal-izations is to rent or buy a tape on deer calling from your local sporting goods store.

Tips for Successful Calling

WEAR a camouflage face mask and gloves while calling. Deer can pinpoint sounds at great distances and easily spot pale or shiny skin (inset).

USE a bleat call when you see a doe in the company of a buck. The bleat may fool the doe into thinking a fawn needs her, and when she comes to investigate, the buck may follow.

BLOW a grunt call when a distant buck is following the scent of a doe. Large, dominant bucks frequently grunt when they are tending a doe in estrus. Mimicking this sound often draws other bucks eager to meet the willing doe.

USE the grunt-snort wheeze call to begin a rattling sequence. This aggressive, challenging call will probably frighten subordinate bucks, but could bring the ultimate macho buck in the neighborhood on the run.

Body Language

When deer are within sight of one another, nearly every movement they make conveys a message to other deer. These cues may signal relaxed contentment, mild alarm, outright panic, dominance or submissiveness.

Hunters who learn to recognize these cues can use the information to their advantage. For example, if you're hunting near a fresh scrape and a medium-sized 8-pointer approaches in a submissive posture, you may decide to pass on harvesting him because a larger, more dominant buck is probably in the area. Some of the most common whitetail body signals are shown below.

Whitetail Body Signals

TAIL WAGGING (left) means the deer is content and senses no danger. A raised tail (center) and intent stare indicate an alert, concerned deer. Any sound or movement will probably cause this animal to bolt. Once the animal is reassured there is no danger, it will lower its tail. Tail flagging (right) means a deer is extremely alarmed. This signal is often seen by hunters who startle and jump bedded or feeding deer.

THE EAR DROP (left) is used by both bucks and does to express aggression, an obvious signal other deer notice almost immediately. During hostile encounters, bucks display dominance (center) by laying ears back, opening eyes wide, flaring nostrils, erecting body hairs (*piloerection*) to increase apparent body size and flattening the tail down against the body. Two bucks in such display approach one another with stiff-legged steps, ready to fight if one does not back down. A subordinate deer (right), tucks its tail between its legs and slinks in a crouch with back depressed or swayed when confronted by a more dominant deer.

Social Organization

Social organization among whitetails is directly related to hierarchy – who is dominant, who is submissive. Dominant deer tend to be healthy animals in the prime of their lives, but patterns of dominance may also be influenced by other factors, particularly the density of the population in which the deer mature. Deer in dense populations spend much of their time competing with each other for food. This competition leads to more struggles for dominance, more complex social interactions and, ultimately, more deaths among subordinate deer. Subordinates in dense populations suffer from stress as a result of their interactions with dominant deer and poorer nutrition as well.

During the fawning period, bucks and does almost never interact, but at many other times of year, the sexes are found in mixed groups. The peak of inter-action comes during the rut, of course, but food brings whitetails together almost as effectively as sex. During summer and early fall, bucks and does commonly feed together in large fields. They stay together all night and split up at first light, the does retiring without male company.

Early fall and winter gatherings of bucks and does on feeding areas are more common in the open farm-land of the Midwest and West than in other parts of whitetail country. Such large mixed groups are prob-ably an adaptation to protect against predators. While the majority of deer in these groups are busy feeding, there are always several sets of eyes and ears on the alert. Winter food shortages also draw bucks and does together around the best forage that's left. In the far North, where winters are very severe, the sexes are forced to aggregate in deer yards in order to conserve energy, find food and avoid predators.

When sexes gather in winter and competition for limited food occurs, aggressive encounters are common. During such interactions, dominant bucks out-compete all other deer; does out-compete fawns, and injured, weak or malnourished deer have the least chance of obtaining food. Where winter food is plentiful, competition is reduced, and bucks and does may not aggregate. In the spring, as snow melts in an area, groups of bucks and does are often seen feeding on south-facing slopes. Then, as all snow disappears and weather improves, the sexes segre-gate into doe and buck groups.

MUTUAL GROOMING (right) is often performed between socially bonded whitetails. Once breeding begins, however, small bucks typically display their subordinant rank by lick-ing the face and forehead of larger, more dominant bucks.

Doe group in fall

Doe Groups

The most common grouping of deer is composed of a dominant doe and one to several generations of her daughters and their fawns. The dominant doe is usually over 3 years old. An experienced mother, she gives her fawns a distinct edge in the game of survival. Her offspring seem to value her skill – as the summer progresses, the matriarch doe and her new family are often joined by her yearling daughters and their fawns. Barren 2-year-old daughters may also join such groups. A daughter that doesn't return to her mother's group will usually establish a home range close by. Yearling sons rarely join such doe groups. They disperse from 1 to 3 miles and establish a new home range in the fall.

Doe groups form and dissolve during the summer and fall. They may separate for days or weeks, then meet again one fine evening on some favored pasture. Does, their fawns and their older daughters all recognize each other. When in the same group or living on adjacent home ranges, they coexist without much antagonistic interaction. If a predator attacks one of their fawns, all may respond.

The first strain on these groups comes during the rut. Some does drive away their fawns during mating season. However, most does tolerate their fawns for about a year, finally driving them away in May, prior to giving birth to another generation of infants. Since these yearlings have been with their mothers for a year, the does often have to resort to aggressive actions to drive them away. After the new fawns are born, a process of imprinting begins immediately. Over several days, does learn to recognize their fawns and vice versa. During imprinting, does become rather territorial, keeping their fawns close and other deer out of the area.

Dominant does bear their fawns in the same general area each year. Their daughters may also use the same area to deliver their fawns. The exception to this behavior may occur in open farm country. One study done in Illinois showed that prior to birthing season, some first-time mothers moved as much as 20 miles to establish home ranges.

Members of a buck group using their forelegs to assert dominance

Buck Groups

Bucks typically are found in groups of two to six members, but larger numbers have been recorded traveling together. They can be seen in each other's company throughout the year, except during the peak of the breeding season, which is when the bucks' testosterone reaches its maximum and the bachelors begin to fight aggressively, establishing and reestablishing a dominance hierarchy. After the does are bred, bucks usually regroup in winter.

It is especially common for several 2½- to 4½-year-old bucks to form social groups. Though floating bucks and younger bucks may temporarily join and spar with members of such groups in the fall, the original bucks in these groups seldom do more than spar. Apparently their day-to-day interactions allow them to determine dominance, thus eliminating the need for serious fighting.

Yearling bucks, which have spent one full year in the care of a doe group, usually live alone after their more dominant mothers force them to leave prior to the breeding season. These bucks are subordinates and may travel several miles before settling into a new home range (p. 59).

Once yearling bucks have established a new home range, they begin to float between groups of does and bucks. They fight very little and stay fat. As a result, the typical yearling that makes it through the hunting season usually survives its first winter on his own. While he is distinctly inferior to adult bucks in his first year, it's a problem that time solves easily enough. After only another year, at 2½, he is ready to become a major player in the social order.

Though yearling bucks may begin to travel with other bucks during the fall, they are inferior to adult bucks and often remain on the periphery of a group's activity. When they interact with larger bucks, they usually pick one of the youngest adults.

Occasionally, a small buck will spar with a tolerant dominant buck. During these rituals, the small buck often shows his subordinate status by licking the face, forehead, neck or shoulders of the larger buck. These

Yearling bucks sparring

encounters with dominant bucks end quickly, and the yearling returns to sparring with bucks his own age (above). As winter progresses, a few yearlings can be seen with their mothers, but most are with unrelated does or with groups of other bucks (see chart below).

From late spring through the breeding season, adult bucks spend half their time alone. When they decide to seek out company during this period, they associate with yearling bucks and other adult bucks equally. During the breeding season, adult bucks are either alone or with does. After the breeding season, most of them are seen in the company of other adult bucks or with does.

Within buck groups, pairs of the largest, most dominant bucks often develop especially close bonds (right). They may leave the larger bachelor groups and travel

A pair of dominant bucks

Comparing Seasonal Groupings of Yearling vs. Adult Bucks *(data from a 1994 Illinois study)*

Yearling Bucks *associated with*	Percentage of Observations		
	April 15-September 30	*October 1-January 15*	*January 15-April 1*
Mother, siblings	33%	7%	10%
Other yearling males	22%	14%	21%
Unrelated does and fawns	22%	33%	37%
Alone	20%	34%	16%
With mature bucks	5%	14%	18%
Adult Bucks			
Mother, siblings	0%	0%	0%
Other yearling males	18%	9%	16%
Unrelated does and fawns	16%	38%	24%
Alone	47%	44%	15%
With mature bucks	19%	8%	43%

together. They can be seen together during the summer and fall, sparring occasionally but mostly just enjoying each other's company. Once the rut starts, they challenge other large bucks in the area until just prior to the peak of the rut, when they separate. These dominant bucks do the lion's share of the mating. But lesser bucks may sneak in to breed a doe while the dominant buck is with another.

The most dominant buck in an area may travel with bachelor groups but more than likely spends most of his time alone. His size and experience allow him to intimidate most competitors and lessen his need to fight. He often covers large areas and may encounter several bachelor herds of bucks. These "top-gun" males may range from 4½ to 8½ years of age. Being at the top, they are constantly tested by other mature bucks (right). Any injury sustained while fighting will lead to their replacement by lesser bucks in the dominance hierarchy.

It is rare for a buck to live past 8½ years in the wild. If he does, he probably loses his top rank, grows smaller antlers, and struggles to regain weight after the rut. Because of his poor physical condition going into winter, he is one of the first to die as the weather sharpens.

In heavily hunted deer herds, a buck over 4 years old is practically unheard of. When bucks are taken by hunters as soon as they develop sizable antlers, 1½- and 2½-year-old bucks do the majority of the breeding. Although these youngsters have less time to test each other, the strongest probably do most of the breeding.

The social interactions between whitetails are complex, but important to ensure that the most adaptive traits are perpetuated in the herd. Their behaviors, signals and hierarchies have evolved for thousands of years, yielding a superior mammal that is well adapted to its environment.

Dominance fights begin with each buck trying to shove the opponent off balance

As the fight continues, the sound of clashing antlers often lures in other bucks

Dominance is established after one buck is defeated and chased off

Deer Movement

Except when they're looking for love, deer move no farther than necessary to find food, water and security. They are expert at hiding in small pockets of cover, which is why they thrive near human activity. Biologists have been able to study deer movements by marking individuals with ear tags or radio collars, then plotting their locations on maps over time. Gradually a pattern of daily and seasonal movements emerges. No amount of study, however, will enable hunters to predict where and when deer will appear at all times. Too many variables tip the odds. Nevertheless, a basic knowledge of deer travel patterns is extremely useful.

Home Range

Although the whole outdoors lies before them, whitetails are not great wanderers. Normally they

live and die within a relatively small home range, rarely leaving it. They eat, sleep and breed in the same places year after year, learning from older deer within that range where to find seasonal foods, shelter from storms and refuge from predators. Even starving deer seldom venture beyond their traditional boundaries.

In a recent Mississippi study, tempting bait stations placed just outside whitetail home ranges could not lure the deer beyond their traditional boundaries. Apparently the security of a well-known home range outweighs the advantages of better forage in a strange land.

The size of a deer's home range varies, depending on habitat. For example, in young deciduous forests where forage and escape cover are both abundant and in close proximity, whitetails do not need to move far to meet their needs. But in open prairie, where a prime, isolated feed field may be several miles from a bedding thicket, they do.

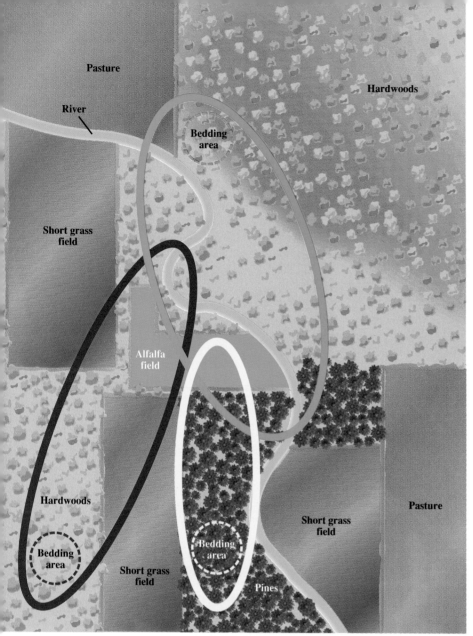

HOME RANGES for most northern whitetails are elliptical in shape because deer usually take the shortest and most efficient routes from bedding to feeding areas.

Home Range Size (acres)

	Spring	Summer	Fall	Winter
Buck fawns	310	160	140	150
Yearling bucks	450	410	675	310
Adult bucks	410	350	1090	290
Doe fawns	390	160	110	275
Yearling does	210	105	260	300
Adult does	190	145	275	400

BUCK AND DOE HOME RANGES vary in size throughout the year. Data from 20 years of radio-tracking in Texas show that adult bucks during fall have the largest home ranges. This is the result of mature bucks traveling through several doe home ranges searching for a doe in estrus.

Home range size also depends on the region of the country in which deer live, the density of the local deer population, the ratios of sex and age in the herd, the time of year and climate. Home ranges can be as small as 100 acres or as large as 2000 acres, but the average is about 1 square mile (640 acres).

Home ranges tend to be larger, more elliptical in shape (left) and less stable in the North than in the South. Cold and snow reduce forage and force deer to search widely for sustenance; thus, the larger size. Dense, brushy thickets are concentrated along narrow river and stream corridors; thus, the elliptical shape. Finally, concentrated and seasonal forage such as a green spring meadow at one end of a territory and a rich fall acorn crop at the other end force deer to change bedding and travel patterns frequently within their larger home ranges; thus, the reduced stability. In the South, habitat is more uniform and consistent; thus, home ranges are smaller, more circular and more stable season to season.

Generally, where the deer population is low, home ranges are large; where the population is high, ranges are small. This is one of those chicken and egg conundrums. Is home range size a result of population size or of the quality of habitat? Probably the latter. The poorer the feeding and hiding cover, the larger the territory needed to survive.

Over the years, tagging and radio collar studies have shown that adult bucks maintain much larger home ranges than do adult does – roughly twice as large.

Yearling bucks tend to have larger home ranges than mature bucks do, because they are subordinate to the larger bucks. Dominant deer command the best habitats and force smaller animals to range more widely in search of feed and cover.

Buck fawns move significantly less than their adult counterparts and are most restricted during the breeding season.

When adult bucks are hunting for does, they may cover three times as much ground as they do at other times of year. Yearling bucks also cover much more country during the breeding season. Does also range more widely at this time, but travel most during winter, apparently to find food. One farm-country study of buck movements during the breeding season came to this conclusion: bucks used 800 acres of their total home range before the breeding season, 1200 acres during it and 1100 acres in winter.

While searching for does in estrus, bucks occasionally foray far afield, sometimes even beyond their normal territorial boundaries. Montana hunters have seen certain trophy bucks move as far as 10 miles from their normal home range in one night, only to return to their original home ranges within 24 hours. This is partly due to the linear nature of river valley habitats in that region.

Dispersal from Home Range

Buck fawns inherit the home range of their dams, but this birthright is short-lived. While a few buck fawns leave their original home range during their first fall, about 75 percent of them will eventually disperse to find new living quarters. At the age of 1½, some of them are forced into leaving during the fall breeding season, both by inattention from the mothers that once doted on them and by big, strange bucks that harass them. The remainder hang around until the following spring when they are again attacked and driven out so that the doe can turn her maternal attentions toward the new fawns she is about to bear.

One interesting study confirms that this occurs. Radio collars were placed on 15 orphaned male fawns and 19 fawns with mothers. Only 9 percent of the orphans later dispersed from the original home range, but 87 percent of those with mothers moved to new home ranges. The average distance traveled was about 5 miles.

Researchers believe there are selective advantages for buck-fawn dispersal. Inbreeding is reduced and genes are spread to new areas. Also, since buck movement is usually from an area of high deer density to one of lower deer density, dispersal may help increase deer numbers in areas where populations are low. Dispersal appears random; fawns wander until they find a place where they are accepted or feel safe.

SCOUT for rubs (above), scrapes, droppings, beds and trails between bedding and feeding sites to identify a buck's home range. Once you are familiar with the area, try to disturb it as little as possible. A mature buck usually won't leave his home range because of hunting pressure, but he will become more nocturnal.

Several studies confirm that yearling buck dispersal occurs. In Virginia, most bucks killed over 1 mile from their home ranges were yearlings, while those killed less than 1 mile from their home ranges averaged over 2½ years of age. In the Midwest, 12 yearling bucks were tagged and subsequently killed by cars. All had dispersed. Seven of those died in October and November, further indication that this is one of the major periods for yearling buck dispersal.

Dispersal isn't limited to yearling bucks. Rarely, older bucks seek new home ranges after they are beaten badly in breeding fights. Sometimes mature bucks drift out of their normal home ranges during the peak of the breeding season, but they return almost immediately thereafter. One Illinois study showed that of 44 bucks aged 2½ years or older, only 3 permanently dispersed from their home range (7 percent).

Trophy buck feeding at sunrise

Daily Movements

Daily movements are affected by light, food, weather, the breeding season and hunting pressure.

LIGHT – Deer are *crepuscular* in their habits, meaning they are most active during early morning (above) and late evening, but they can adjust this schedule in reaction to food availability, hunting pressure or weather. Deer spend much of their time reclining while chewing their cud from foods eaten during the night. Beds are usually positioned in dense cover where air currents carry the scent of approaching predators. Though most deer commonly bed in the same general vicinity, they seldom lie in exactly the same spot. As evening descends, deer rise and move toward feeding areas, traveling from a few hundred yards to as many as several miles to reach them. They spend the night feeding and resting on the feed grounds, then return to heavy cover early the next morning.

FOOD – For much of the breeding season, bucks are more interested in mating than eating, but from summer through early October, their lives revolve around food. They spend many hours in soybean and corn fields, where available. One 3-year-old, radio-collared buck in Illinois farm country remained in corn, soybean and other crop fields for an entire month during late summer. Another 4-year-old buck was tracked for 24 straight hours on several days. One day he spent 22 hours in the corn. Another day he spent 21 hours there. During hot summer days, bucks move little and may use but a few acres of their home ranges. Standing corn and other lush crops provide not only food but also excellent cover in summer. The average distance from bedding areas to crop fields in farm country is about 500 yards. Does and fawns bed closest; bucks bed slightly farther away. Hunters do well by watching trails between feeding and bedding sites.

When crops are harvested and fields stripped bare, deer are forced to move to nearby hedgerows, woods, brushy stream valleys, cattail sloughs and similar undisturbed cover. They may still feed in the open fields, but they'll travel through some kind of cover whenever possible. When  crops are plowed under or buried by snow, whitetails switch to woody browse, dried and cured herbaceous plants, and mast, especially acorns (above).

WEATHER – Temperature is the single most important weather phenomenon influencing deer movement. When it's hot, whitetails wait until the cooler periods from dusk to dawn to move. To beat the heat, they lie quietly in cool, shady areas such as dense hardwoods and conifers, along stream bottoms, in or near wetlands or in brushy areas.

As temperatures cool in fall, deer begin to move earlier in the afternoons and later in the mornings. During the cold of winter, they may be forced to feed actively in broad daylight to maintain body condition. When temperatures drop below 0 degrees Fahrenheit, they move as little as necessary to conserve energy, often bedding right where they feed, especially on south-facing slopes or in areas protected from bitter winds. When they do move, it tends to be at the warmest part of the day.

Approaching storms often stimulate prolonged feeding. Some suspect whitetails can detect changing barometric pressure, but this has not been proven. The reduced light of heavy cloud cover may encourage earlier movement to feeding grounds.

Deer often feed right through a snow or light rain (above right), but heavy precipitation and high winds force them into cover. In the South, cold, damp weather throws a wet blanket on deer activity. Once a storm passes, feeding again increases unless snow has piled deep. Deer may stay in bed for extended periods after a heavy snowfall, particularly if the mercury plummets.

Whitetails seem to become more active in light breezes, perhaps because they then feel confident about identifying predators by scent (right). However, several studies show that when winds are above 14 mph, deer movement decreases. Deer become skittish as noisy gusts interfere with their ability to smell or hear. Other studies, however, indicate that a few bucks break with tradition and actually move more during big blows. One Texas study found that whitetails "buddy up" to increase their ability to detect predators during high winds.

Whitetail moving during light rain

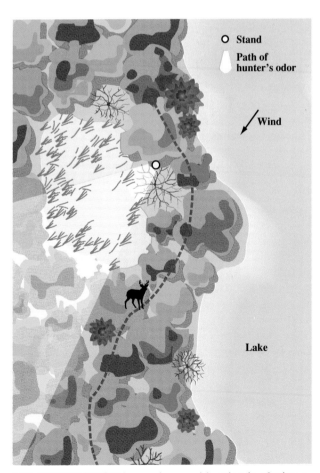

WIND DIRECTION is a major consideration in placing a stand. A good rule of thumb is to set the stand so deer pass your stand using a quartering wind. This way, they will move with confidence by relying on their sense of smell to detect danger ahead and miss your odor trail.

In the far north and in western mountains, deer respond to deep snow (right), cold and limited food by migrating from summer to winter ranges (far right). These migrations occur in isolated areas as far south as Missouri, but more commonly in northern portions of Michigan, Minnesota, Wisconsin, North and South Dakota and Idaho.

These migrations usually occur in late November and early December. Distances traveled are usually 10 to 30 miles, but one herd in Minnesota moved an incredible 55 miles.

In spring, does return to summer range first. Both sexes often migrate in fits and stops as they move toward summer pastures, then drift back when a spring storm hits, only to try again as weather improves. In South Dakota, spring migration began in mid-April and was completed by mid-May. But in the northern Black Hills, deer rushed from winter to summer range in less than 2 days. Various studies have shown that individual whitetails use the same summer and winter ranges from year to year, probably after learning them from older deer with which they associated as fawns and yearlings.

In northern forests, deer often congregate in traditional areas known as *yards*. These areas provide shelter from severe winter conditions, and deer will move to the same one each year. White cedar swamps and areas with stands of jack pine, balsam fir, red spruce and hemlock are selected. Often the yards are located near streams or wetlands. Deer prefer yards with good tree growth and mature conifers, which provide almost three-fourths canopy cover. These yards provide cover from winds and protection from snow pack and drifting snows. Hemlock and cedar are preferred foods quickly eaten in the yards. Then deer feed on maples, black cherry, dogwood and other woody browse on the outskirts of the deer yard.

Deer do not stay in the yards in years when winters are mild. During severe winters deer remain in the yards for up to 5 months, and they will not leave even when foods are in minimal supply. The reasons for this are complex. Some believe that deer yards evolved as a way to reduce wolf predation. But most importantly, they help the animals conserve energy,

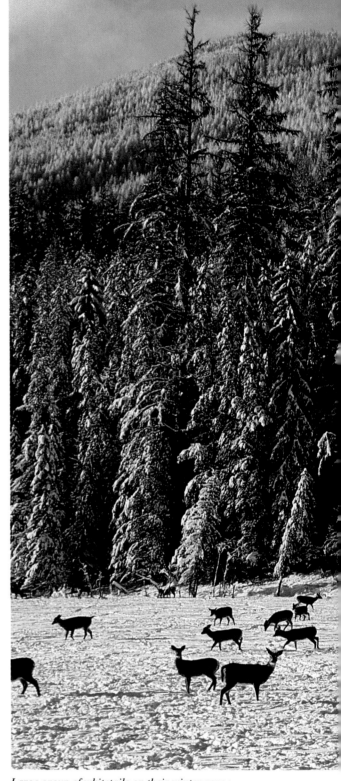

Large group of whitetails on their winter range

especially during very cold weather. Apparently they can survive such conditions, even with little food, by remaining in the deer yards.

BREEDING SEASON – Early in the breeding season, most yearling deer disperse to new areas. Deer seem to disappear from alfalfa fields and other open areas where they were commonly seen before. They continue to feed in these areas, but become more nocturnal, especially in areas where hunter densities

are higher. When this happens, hunters must move away from field edges and get closer to bedding sites or feeding areas in the woods interior.

Bucks move more during the breeding season than at any other time of the year. With does it is often the opposite. The closer the doe gets to the time of conception, the less she moves. The belief is that a doe has a better chance of attracting a buck by putting down more odor in a small area than by wandering around in a larger one. The doe comes into heat, urinates in scrapes and stays close to that area, making her more easily found by the buck.

Although the doe moves less during the early part of the breeding season, research done in Virginia shows that, once the buck finds and begins to follow an estrus doe, she spends more time moving. Apparently, the constant attention given by a tending buck causes her to spend more time on her feet than usual.

Tending buck watches as a doe in estrus feeds

When the estrus doe is not quite receptive, a buck may follow her for several days. She will stop to feed on occasion, but the buck rarely feeds at this time (above). Some researchers speculate that this continued movement over several days tests the stamina of the buck, ensuring that only the most physically healthy animals will mate does.

Because bucks are focusing much less on food and more on reproduction during the fall, areas with scrapes and rub lines become excellent places for hunters to look for bucks. Other good hunting locations are funnel areas, places where open fields, lakes or large rivers force deer to travel through narrow corridors. Intersections where two or three cover types come together, but which also have fence lines, streams, field edges or old trails, are also excellent locations for hunters to place stands.

After the majority of the does have been bred, buck movement becomes a bit less focused on reproduction, but does are still important. Hunters who use the combined methods of intercepting deer between bedding and feeding areas as well as hunting scrape

and rub lines are often the most successful. In much of the North, snow now covers the forest floor, making it easy to determine trails and routes used by deer.

HUNTING PRESSURE – Hunted deer rarely leave their normal home range. Studies show that, even if nonhuntable refuges are adjacent to deer range, most deer will not move there. Nonhuntable refuges might be a state park, a National Wildlife Refuge or just a tract of land that is not open to hunting. Deer that have a portion of their home range within such a refuge may go there when hunting pressure gets heavy (opposite page). Some does whose range lies outside such refuges will move onto an adjacent unhunted refuge for short periods. But bucks will not leave their home range and go to such refuges, even when pressured. Instead, they will seek thick cover within their home range. When they have a direct encounter with a hunter, after an initial short run, they move slowly rather than attract attention.

If a buck has a home range within an unhunted refuge, he will keep almost all of his activities within that

Relocating Whitetails

Over the years deer have been moved from their home range to other areas to reestablish populations and to remove excess deer from suburban areas (right). In one northern Minnesota study, 9 deer were relocated 6 to 14 miles from their home range in winter. One traveled 11 miles directly away from its original home and was killed by a wolf 35 days after release. Another was killed by a wolf 3 days after release. A female and her male fawn returned to their original home range. Another adult female moved in the direction of her home range but was killed by a wolf about 6 miles short of her destination. A female fawn moved halfway home, then stopped and went to a new home range. Three other deer established new home ranges.

Most studies done on deer that have been trapped and relocated show that mortality of such deer is quite high. For this reason, some states do not allow the trapping and relocating of deer from areas of high deer populations because such movement is inhumane. In those situations, other alternatives are then sought to lower deer populations (see Populations, p. 29).

refuge. If the buck does leave the refuge, he will only do so at night.

When a hunter jumps a deer, it will run hard for as much as ½ mile in open habitat, but usually less than 200 yards in thick cover. In heavy cover, deer will often run a short distance, then utilize known trails to slowly take them into a safe area. Often they double back. This is probably not done to outsmart the hunter, but rather because the deer does not want to leave its home range.

A prime example of the whitetail's ability to avoid hunters occurred in Michigan. In this case study, six hunters were given a 1-square-mile enclosure to hunt seven resident bucks. It took them 124 hours of hunting just to see one buck!

Whitetails hide from their predators by either lying low, or by using all their instincts and abilities to secretly travel throughout their home range. No other big game animal is more successful than the whitetail in moving about undetected, and that makes pursuing them the ultimate challenge for many hunters.

Group of deer in a nonhuntable refuge

Breeding

The rut is an exciting time to be in the woods. There's more happening among whitetails now than at any other time of year – sparring, chasing, fighting, calling, rubbing and scraping among the bucks and an exceptional amount of movement even among does and fawns. That's probably why hunters and researchers alike have spent more time studying the behavior of whitetails in rut than they have spent understanding the breeding rituals of any other big game animal.

The whitetail breeding season can be divided into three distinct periods: *pre-rut* – the 1 to 2 months of rubbing, scraping and chasing that occur before the females are bred; *rut* – the few weeks when the vast majority of breeding takes place; and *post-rut* – the month or more in which bucks recover from the rigors of the pre-rut and rut but still actively breed any females that come into estrus.

The three breeding periods occur when shorter days of fall stimulate hormonal flow and behaviors that conclude with the successful insemination of does. As a rule, the timing of these periods begins about a month earlier in the North than the South. For example, in Montana, Minnesota and Wisconsin, most does are bred in November; in South Texas and Mississippi, mid-December to mid-January. There are exceptions, however, due to climate and localized factors such as flooding. In South Florida, for example, breeding begins in August; in coastal areas of Georgia, early October.

In general, the whitetail breeding season tends to last longer in the South than the North. This is due primarily to the increased survival rate of fawns that have been born unusually early or late, which in turn begin to breed.

The Pre-Rut Period

The pre-rut period generally has two phases. In most of the northern part of the whitetail's range, the first phase begins when bucks shed velvet in early September and runs to the third week in October. During the early first phase, bucks have regular travel routines. They show little interest in females but may make some tree rubs.

The second phase runs from about October 20 to November 10. Many hunters call it the "peak of the rut." Among bucks, it is a time for making rubs and scrapes, sparring, leaving pheromones from their scents glands where other deer will find them, stimulating females, and challenging and intimidating other bucks. It is a time when bucks are very interested in females.

Bucks commonly spar during the pre-rut period – one buck lowers his head to "present" antlers to a rival, and the rival responds by dropping his head and making contact with his antlers. It is more pushing and shoving than fighting and is not highly aggressive. Sparring bucks twist their heads and often appear to be playing as they push each other around. Sparring usually involves bucks of different sizes (below). Smaller bucks initiate sparring with larger bucks. The smaller buck will lick the forehead or nose of the larger buck (a submissive behavior), then begin to push and shove. This can go on for 15 to 20 minutes with periodic breaks in the action.

A large buck sparring with a smaller buck

Such sparring is very ritualized – when a small buck breaks off the contest, the larger buck lets him escape. This etiquette gives small bucks a chance to learn to fight without getting hurt, and it helps them learn to gauge an opponent's strength by associating the size of his antlers and body with the size of his wallop. During the pre-rut, sparring matches do not lead to clear winners or losers, but bucks do use them to begin establishing dominance.

Sparring has two peaks in the northern United States. The first is around mid-October, and the second around mid-November. Before mid-October, over three-fourths of all sparring is done by larger bucks, but after that, smaller bucks do most of the sparring. And during the rut period, almost all sparring is done by small bucks. Bigger bucks are mating with females during this time.

Buck following a doe in estrus

Two mature bucks fighting

"Scramble" fighting can also occur during the pre-rut. A scramble is not ritualized. It is a simple fight but not highly aggressive. Two, three or even four younger bucks may join in a "scramble." Injuries can occur during scrambles, but observations suggest that it is not important to the individual whether he loses or not.

Mock fights also occur during the pre-rut period. These fights are similar to sparring but more intense. These pushing matches do lead to a winner, with the loser submissively leaving the area.

Although sparring is much more common than aggressive fights, serious fights do occur. These fights are usually caused by access to estrus females. When an estrus female attracts two dominant bucks, a very aggressive fight can occur. The size of a buck's antlers and his weight influence his chances in one of these struggles. Bigger is nearly always better. His position in the dominance ranking will make a difference as well. If he has beaten his opponent in a casual sparring match earlier in the season, he will probably prevail in a serious fight as well.

There are some ritualized behaviors as the two bucks approach each other, but once the fight starts, the test of dominance begins (above). Equally matched bucks will fight until one tires or takes advantage of topography to gain an advantage. Such fights may last for as long as 30 minutes, but most are shorter,

brutal battles. Once the loser gives up, he quickly turns and escapes, with the aggressor in hot pursuit. If possible, the winner will inflict a hard antler jab to the rear of the retreating animal.

Often these fights result in broken antlers, eye injuries, torn ears, broken shoulders and deep puncture wounds. One study of tanned deer skins showed that the average buck suffers 24 wounds to its body each year. The most common buck wounds are found on the neck (right).  Apparently some bucks are more aggressive than others – they carry the scars of many more puncture wounds than rivals of the same age. Only 1 percent of these wounds are visible on live deer in the wild.

Dominant bucks wear themselves out fighting and chasing does during the breeding season. By early winter, they have lost body fat and weight. Some will look thin, and biologists suggest that they suffer the aftereffects of wounds obtained while fighting.

An exhausted buck tries to free his locked antlers from those of his dead opponent

The most active breeding bucks suffer most. Their weight loss and injuries during the fall come at a critical time, just as the rigors of winter set in. If the winter is hard, many of the most dominant bucks will die. It is also possible during aggressive fights for mature bucks to get their antlers locked, leading to the death of one or both combatants (above). This is rare, but it happens.

Bucks and does remain separate for most of the year. However, during the breeding season, they must find each other for courtship and breeding. Bucks use rubs and scrapes as *scent posts* to communicate with each other and with does. Rubs and scrapes are easy for hunters to find but often difficult to understand. A knowledge of these signposts is imperative if you are to understand the world of the whitetail.

Large buck rubbing a sapling

RUBS. Rubs are first made during the pre-rut period and although scientists (and hunters) know a lot about rubbing behavior, there is much we still do not know.

For years people thought that bucks "rubbed" to remove velvet from their antlers or as practice for combat later in the fall. Neither is true. Bucks do rub their antlers on trees, shrubs, brush, etc., when the velvet begins to dry and peel in September, but biologists don't think "itchy velvet" is the reason for the rubs.

In the 1960s, scientists observed bucks rubbing the same tree in successive years and suggested that they were marking territories. More recent observation suggests that this isn't true either. Although the function of rubs is still not totally understood, we do know that they are a form of communication between bucks and between sexes. Though dominant bucks leave scent on rubs that lesser bucks recognize and avoid, such bucks do not "defend" these areas as

true territories. In fact, many mature and lesser bucks may use the same area and rub the same trees.

Most rubbing occurs in the pre-rut period. When making rubs, a buck stands with antlers against a tree and pushes up, down or sideways. A careful look at a rub can tell a hunter something about the size of the buck that created it. The gnarly, rough antler bases typical of older bucks will leave deep groves in the bark of the tree. It is sometimes possible to determine how wide and high the antlers are by examining trees and shrubs that are adjacent to the tree being rubbed. While rubbing his antler bases on the tree of his choice, a buck with large antlers may damage adjacent trees and shrubs with his tines.

The average time a buck spends making a rub can vary, but the initial scraping of bark by antlers can be accomplished in just 15 seconds. Animals typically rub for a few seconds, then stop to sniff and lick the bark they have rubbed. One buck may make as many as 30 to 40 rubs in a morning and make 300 rubs during one breeding season. There are two factors that are known to determine the density of rubs in an area. The more older bucks in an area, the more rubs. And timber that produces a lot of acorns also has more rubs than timber that is acorn-poor.

The very first rubs of the season appear in September and early October. There are few of them, and studies show that they are made by dominant bucks. Such rubs may be used again as the breeding season develops. Such rubs are a clue to the hunter that a dominant buck is using this area. In areas where the deer herd is hunted very heavily (many eastern states) and there are few older bucks, rubbing is delayed until mid- to late October.

Both bucks and does have a scent gland about halfway up their forehead (p. 17). It is especially prominent in bucks during the pre-rut and rut period, and, on many bucks, distinctly different hair color makes this gland easily visible. Close observations of bucks making tree rubs show that they rub the forehead gland on the newly opened, moist bark. They often leave hair on the bark along with the scent. The amount of scent the forehead gland produces correlates with the social status and age of the animal. Dominant bucks more than $2\frac{1}{2}$ years old secrete more forehead scent than do their younger counterparts.

Dominant females may also rub their foreheads on buck rubs, and dominant females sniff and nibble the rubs, too. Clearly there is something there that interests big bucks and the dominant females that get bred first.

Other behaviors have been seen at buck rubs. One study noted that bucks and does touched the rubs

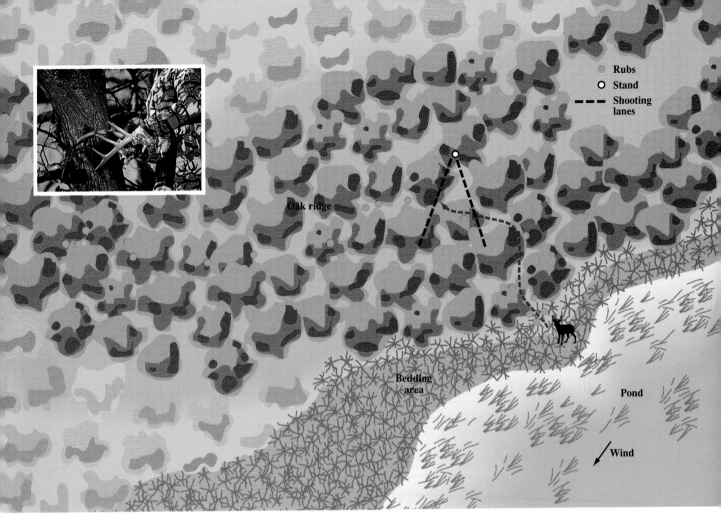

RATTLING (inset) works best during the later stages of the pre-rut period. For best results, set up a stand along rub lines between bedding and feeding areas. Search for these rub lines on oak ridges where deer are feeding heavily on acorns.

with their rumps. No further studies have focused on this interesting behavior.

Some studies show that deer tend to rub red cedars, sumac, sassafras and other aromatic trees and shrubs. The supposition is that these trees allow a better deposit of deer scent. Some researchers challenge the notion that deer prefer to rub heavily scented trees, but there is no debate on the notion that tree rubs are very important markers that help deer communicate during the breeding season.

Rubs are often made in a line along a trail, each rub being visible to deer walking along that trail. In fact, hunters have "moved" deer trails closer to their tree stands by using a deer antler or folding saw to make a series of rubs. As bucks move to and from feeding areas in the morning and evening, they often walk along a trail, stop and make a rub, then travel on. In such situations, a hunter can figure out which way the deer was moving by noting which side of the tree has been rubbed.

In October, many smaller bucks leave their home ranges and disperse into new areas. This is why hunters begin to see large numbers of small rubs scattered throughout the woods in October. For a hunter, these rubs simply mean that many smaller bucks are on the move. It is unlikely that these rubs will be revisited by bucks or does, so there is little point in setting up a stand to watch one.

There is another kind of rub that is very important to bucks, does and hunters. This is the "traditional rub" made on the same tree year after year. Traditional rubs are almost always found on large trees, which indicates that larger bucks are doing the rubbing. They are often made on aromatic trees such as cedars. Research shows that traditional rubs are very important for dominant bucks. Though smaller bucks will visit these rubs during daylight, and there is some use by big bucks at dusk, most mature bucks only visit traditional rubs at night. Thus, to hunt such rubs, a hunter should set up a distance from the rub along a likely trail, hoping that a buck will move to or from the rub while there is shooting light. It's a long shot, but the chances are improved by the fact that more than one mature buck may visit a traditional rub. In fact, some such rubs are used by many mature bucks. Bucks use these rubs throughout the pre-rut, rut and post-rut, but the highest use is during the actual breeding period for females.

Buck urinating over his tarsal glands

Buck scent-marking the overhead branch

SCRAPES. The second kind of whitetail scent post is the *scrape*. Scrapes attract females, serve as locations where one buck can intimidate another, establish dominance among males, indicate a buck's presence to other bucks and does, indicate his readiness to breed and indicate the female's readiness to breed.

Where deer densities are high, the buck-to-doe ratio may be as high as 1:8 and a buck may not need to leave scrapes to find a doe in estrus. But where the buck-to-doe ratio is 1:2 or 1:3, scraping will usually be intense.

Observers of deer behavior have created elaborate classifications for scrapes, but all the categories can be lumped into two major groups – scrapes made once and not revisited (*nonactive scrapes*) and "hot" scrapes that convey a great deal of scent and meaning to deer and become a focus for breeding activity (*active scrapes*). Nonactive scrapes can be found randomly scattered along game trails, old roads, small openings and woods borders, especially at intersections of deer trails around fields. Such scrapes are probably made by wandering smaller bucks moving to and from feeding, or dispersing from their home range. These scrapes provide no advantage for hunters, because they occur randomly and will not be revisited by does or bucks.

Before a buck makes a scrape, he may urinate on his tarsal glands (above left). During normal urination, the buck stands with hind legs apart. But, when he intends to make a scrape, he keeps the hind legs together so that urine reaches the tarsal glands, located on the inside of the leg (this behavior is referred to as *rub-urination*). Often the buck will then lick the inside of his hind legs.

The combination of urine and tarsal scent really smells. As he walks he may lick or pull on low branches with his mouth. He also may run his antlers and forehead in such overhanging limbs. This puts more of his scent in the area.

All active scrapes involve an overhanging branch (left). Once a buck marks a branch, he will paw the ground under it, making two to five strokes with each front foot (opposite page). The oval-shaped scrape usually measures about 2 to 3 feet long. The final behavior of scrape making is urination in or around the scrape.

It is probably true that younger bucks make smaller scrapes. Younger bucks don't usually revisit their scrapes, so they remain small, while mature bucks come back to active scrapes again and again, pawing and scenting each time, enlarging the scrape with each visit.

SCRAPES are made by bucks raking away grass, leaves and twigs with their front hooves. These oval-shaped patches of bare dirt are easily found by hunters (inset).

There is debate on how a scrape is opened. Some suggest that dominant bucks first open up a scrape. Many others believe that dominant does urinate on an area that was used as a hot scrape the previous year. Then a buck in that vicinity makes a scrape on that spot and urinates in it as a marker. Soon other does and bucks are also visiting the area. Regardless of what sex opens a scrape, it is the older bucks that first use hot scrapes, some 2 months before the peak of breeding occurs.

Finding active scrapes that are used by bucks and does during the pre-rut period can give hunters an advantage. These scrapes are usually in open woods with little understory, close to heavy cover. Stream bottoms adjacent to hawthorn thickets are favored scrape spots. One study showed that scrapes and rubs are often clustered together. Deer may open active scrapes early in September, but most do not appear until mid-October.

As bucks and does visit an active scrape, trails begin to develop. Some evolve into a pattern that resembles a wheel, with the hub being the scrape. Activity at

these scrapes will vary, but peak activity will usually occur during the last week of October and the first week of November. Once actual breeding starts in mid-November, activity around scrapes quickly dies down.

It appears that dominant bucks may use the same scrape location from one year to the next. These scrapes are the equivalent of "traditional rubs." They are hot spots for big bucks. No one knows why the deer reopen these scrapes in successive years. Some suggest that the dominant buck visits these sites in the summer and scent-marks the overhanging branches. Others suggest that, after a buck meets an estrus doe at a scrape, he opens a scrape on the same spot in following years. Still others suggest that dominant females open such scrapes at the same spots where they bred the previous season. One thing is sure – they are reopened year after year.

Deer may visit an active scrape several days in a row, then neglect it for a week. Dominant bucks in the area will continue to visit a hot scrape well past the peak of doe estrus. Since unbred females come

Scrape-Hunting Tips

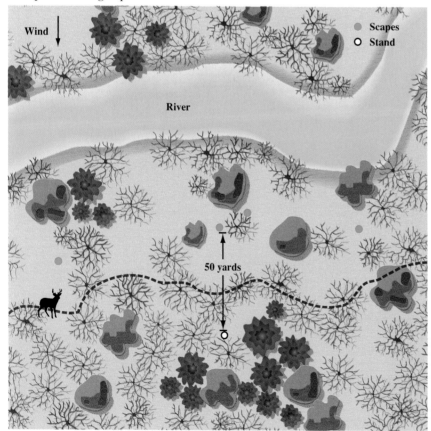

PLACE your stand 40 to 60 yards downwind of a scrape line instead of right on top of a single scrape. Bucks often scent-check scrapes from downwind rather than walk right through them. This is especially true if the scrapes are in fairly open terrain and thicker cover lies to the downwind side.

COVER a scrape with leaves to determine if it is being revisited by bucks. If the leaves are not pawed out in a few days, the buck isn't actively using it.

into estrus every 25 to 27 days, these females may continue to visit and urinate in active scrapes, thus stimulating bucks to visit them as well. Regardless of what the stimulus for such visits is, bucks have been known to visit active scrapes 3 months after the peak of estrus.

Behavior of does and bucks at the scrape could fill a textbook. Smaller bucks often smell the scrape and any nearby tree rubs from a distance of several feet, then become submissive and leave the area. Often these bucks will not paw or urinate in the scrape. A mature buck may smell and/or lick the overhanging limb. He may rub his forehead gland or the gland at the corner of his eye on the limb as well. The belief is that the preorbital gland in the corner of the eye plays a role in deer communication. Other scent may also be left on the limb. Nasal oil gland secretions and saliva may be left on overhanging limbs.

After extensive smelling and licking of the overhanging limb, the buck will smell and paw the scrape, then urinate in it. Females also visit the scrapes. They may lick and smell the overhanging limbs. They also will smell the scrape and on rare occasions will actually paw the scrape.

Subordinate bucks are not only uneasy around existing scrapes, but they make fewer scrapes of their own. When there are few old bucks in an area, the young bucks will make scrapes. However, they scrape much less than mature bucks.

Observations of deer by researchers show that there are three peak visitation periods at scrapes. The strongest occurs from 8:45 A.M. to 10:15 A.M.; the second strongest, from 3:45 P.M. to 5:15 P.M.; and the least intense peak, from 11:45 A.M. to 1:15 P.M. Interestingly, more females visit scrapes in the early morning and more bucks visit from 9:00 A.M. to 10:15 A.M.

Scraping activity increases dramatically in late October and probably peaks the first week of November. The amount of scraping is reduced once the peak of the rut, and mating, is reached. However, bucks will continue to visit scrapes every few days clear through February. Bucks often visit scrapes to "rescent" them with urine after it rains or snows.

Apparently scrapes serve as spots where bucks can locate, then follow, females coming into estrus. Often bucks will not come to the scrape, but rather move downwind. This allows them to scent an estrus doe without placing themselves in danger by coming to the scrape. However, one study showed that during the late afternoon, bucks will usually come to the scrape rather than stay downwind. There is no explanation for this behavior.

How to Make a Mock Scrape

CUT a long sapling with a pruning shear. Wear rubber gloves to avoid leaving scent. Trim the sapling so the tips are about ½ inch in diameter.

TIE the sapling with twine so its tips are about 5 feet above the ground. This sapling will serve as the overhead branch for the mock scrape.

RAKE away leaves, twigs and grass in an oblong from 2 to 3 feet long. Do this directly under the overhead branch. Drip buck tarsal gland scent (inset) or doe-in-estrus scent into the exposed dirt of the mock scrape.

A tending buck (right) lowers his ears to challenge an intruder (middle)

The Rut Period

Whitetail breeding activity begins as the females approach estrus, or "heat." The doe estrus cycle can vary from 21 to 30 days, but 25 to 27 days is the most common interval. Does in captivity have been known to have as many as seven estrus cycles in a year, but in the wild, a doe that is not bred is likely to have three or four cycles during the fall and early winter.

Female fawns and yearlings reach estrus later than mature females. In the North, about 80 percent of adult females are bred during the mid-November estrus, and by mid-December nearly all females are bred.

For bucks, rutting behavior is triggered by the shorter days of fall. Because latitude affects day length, the rut begins early in the North (about the middle of November) and progressively later as you move south. In warmer climates, the rutting season may not begin until mid-January. Genetics and regional variations can also affect the starting date of the rut.

In females, a surge of estrogen triggers nocturnal activity just prior to mating. Although the doe is receptive to bucks for only about 24 hours, she attracts males for about 3 days. Biologists believe that estrus females probably release vaginal discharges that help attract bucks. When the doe is ready to breed, she urinates in an active scrape and these odors, with others, cause the dominant buck to seek her. The buck tends the doe for 1 to 2 days, until she becomes passive and allows the buck to mate with her.

In areas where deer populations are high and there is a high doe-to-buck ratio, bucks find it easy to locate ready females. Under these circumstances, bucks are less likely to visit scrapes. In areas with high deer numbers, females tend to breed several weeks later, either because there are not enough bucks, or because competition for food has left the females poorly nourished. Fawns born to late-breeding females have a more difficult time – they are born later in the spring, which means they are smaller when the next winter comes around. It's a subtle difference, but one that often means an early death for the late-born.

Other factors may influence the rut. An approaching cold front in late October or late November can hasten and intensify the rut. It was once believed that the sudden drop in temperature caused by such a

LOCATE a doe group during the rut period, and wait for bucks to show up checking for a doe in estrus. Mature bucks usually visit several doe groups each day, so when a doe from the group is ready to breed, you'll practically be guaranteed a chance at a quality buck.

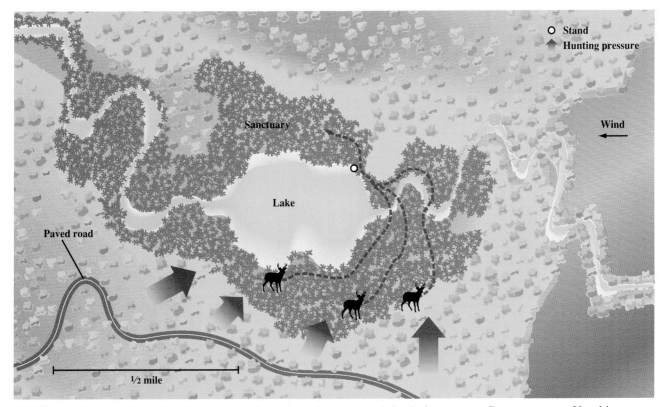

PLAN on moderate to heavy hunting pressure throughout the rut, especially during an open firearms season. Use this to your advantage by stand-hunting along deer escape routes leading to sanctuaries.

The Moon and Movement of Deer during the Rut

For generations, hunters and biologists have speculated on the relationship between the full moon and deer movement. The most basic notion is that the full moon prompts deer to feed more at night. Thus, it's better to hunt during the new moon, when deer are more active during the day. Many hunters have kept extensive data on deer sightings during the full moon. Some show more deer seen, others show fewer. Scientific research on deer activity during the full moon is also a mixed bag. Some studies show more deer activity and movement during a full moon; other studies show less.

There are more complex theories as well. One is that the timing of the new moon can change the peak breeding time for females. It takes note of the fact that, as days become shorter, the whitetail doe releases sex hormones and goes into estrus. Supporters of this theory believe that the doe responds to a decrease in moonlight as well as sunlight. If the new moon comes during the beginning of the peak reproductive period, the doe will be exposed to less light during the night as well as during the day. As a result, the thinking goes, some breeding will be earlier than normal. This then makes the breeding period longer than normal, maybe as much as 2 weeks in length. Since the females are in heat longer, the intensity of breeding behavior should not be as high as when the new moon comes at the beginning of the normal breeding period, but it will be nice and steady and much longer.

If the new moon comes late in the breeding period, does will breed later than normal. This "new moon-reduced light" theory has not been scientifically proven, but it is an interesting idea. It could explain why peak rutting activity might vary by a few days from one year to the next in the same area.

There is a second new theory concerning the way the moon may control deer movements that relates to moon characteristics other than moon phase. This theory considers distance to the moon (which changes each day), moon declination (the position of the moon's orbit over your hunting location, which changes daily and varies with latitude) and the percent of illumination. It notes that all full moons are not alike because declination can make one full moon brighter than another. This could explain why some studies show more deer movement during full moon and others show less movement. Supporters of this theory speculate that all of these moon characteristics interact in a complicated and unexplainable way to affect deer movements. Using a computer and data for all moon characteristics, one can predict during which days of the pre-rut, rut, and post-rut the deer will be most active.

Many factors influence deer movement during the rut, including temperature change, rain, barometric pressure, wind and number of hunters. But it seems very likely that characteristics of the moon, including moon phase, play a role that is not yet fully understood.

cold front was responsible for such accelerated breeding behavior, but recent research suggests that the cloudy, dark days associated with bad weather are actually responsible for triggering rut activity.

Heavy hunting of adult bucks seems to have little effect on female breeding success. In some states, such as Pennsylvania and West Virginia, more than 70 percent of adult bucks are harvested each fall, but while surviving bucks may be very young in such areas, nearly all adult females breed successfully. Studies have shown that, when mature bucks are missing, the yearling bucks generally manage to impregnate all available does, even though these young suitors tend to exhibit less courtship behavior and engage in less rub-and-scrape activity than older bucks.

Because bucks are often less wary while they are pursuing does, some observers have suggested that bucks are very vulnerable to hunters during the rut. While there is no doubt that the rut does improve the hunter's odds of harvesting a buck, most older bucks manage to avoid being shot during the rut by adopting a simple strategy – they do most of their doe chasing at night.

The Post-Rut Period

The post-rut period extends from the time the main breeding period ends in mid- to late November until the bucks lose their antlers. In most areas, the gun hunting season is closed during most of the post-rut, but late bow seasons often provide hunting opportunities during this period.

Does that were not bred in the major estrus period will recycle during the post-rut and come into heat a second time. This is more common in areas with very dense populations of deer, and high doe-

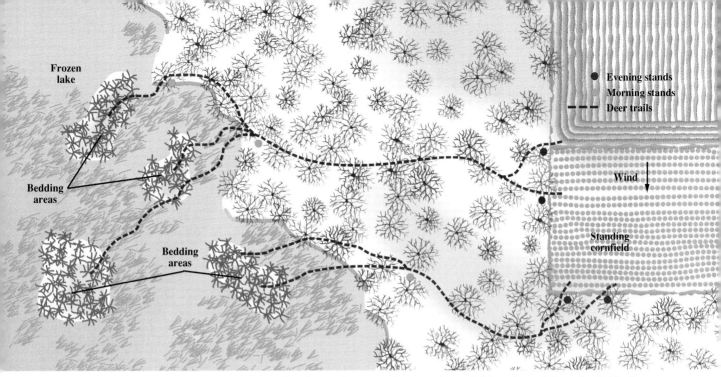

IDENTIFY the main food source for post-rut whitetails, such as an unharvested cornfield, and stand-hunt the field edges or along trails leading to the bedding areas. Rattling, calling and scrape-hunting may work in the post-rut, but not as well as during the pre-rut or rut.

to-buck ratios. If there is plenty of deer food and fawns reach the fall in good condition, as many as 80 percent of all doe fawns will come into estrus in the post-rut period. This is especially true in the farm country of the Midwest and portions of southern deer range. Where snows are heavy, fawn pregnancy rates are low. This is probably because fawns must concentrate on survival and evolution would work against those that had the extra burden of pregnancy.

Fawns that become pregnant give birth to single fawns, rather than twins, and their estrus periods are much longer than the 2 to 3 days of adult does. In northern habitats, the survival of fawns born to fawns is lower because the second generation of fawns is dropped later in the spring. This means that they enter the winter weighing less than counterparts born to adult does. In the southern habitats, where breeding seasons are naturally a bit late, fawns born to fawns have a higher rate of survival.

The late-season estrus of fawns and adult does stimulates bucks to visit rubs and scrapes periodically but with much less attention than they exhibited in the main breeding period. In areas with a healthy herd and a low doe-to-buck ratio, breeding activity is generally greatly reduced in the post-rut when compared to the main estrus period. In areas where there is a high doe-to-buck ratio, there is more breeding (but still greatly reduced) during the post-rut period. Though bucks are capable of breeding through the winter, their physical condition deteriorates during the main rut, and they begin to lose interest in seeking the does.

The post-rut period is usually a colder time for deer in most of their range. Since they need more energy to maintain their body temperature during the deepening cold of December, they spend more time feeding. Though bucks may still chase females, they typically spend more time feeding and resting.

In much of the country, most bucks are harvested during the pre-rut and rut periods. Even so, some really trophy bucks are still available to the serious hunter during the post-rut. There are some things hunters can do to increase their odds during the late season. Use aerial photos and study your hunting areas. Also study the hunters that hunt in your area. Focus on areas that other hunters miss. Pick out several areas you feel may harbor bucks and hunt each one. Use late-season snows to help you find deer bedding cover, main feeding areas (above) and the important travel lanes. Finally, spend lots of time in the woods and your post-rut hunting experiences should improve.

The whitetail breeding season offers a hunter opportunities he doesn't have at other times of the year. Because bucks are seeking each other out to establish their dominance, a hunter can improve his chances with calls and rattling. Because bucks trail estrus does like a beagle trailing a rabbit, a hunter can improve his chances with deer scents. Because bucks chase does, a hunter can improve his chances with a decoy. There are certainties in nature that are important for humans in such an uncertain world. The breeding season is one of the certainties of nature . . . and it can help you find the trophy you're after.

Trophy Bucks

Producing Trophy Bucks

Antlers have always fascinated humans. Before we could write, we were painting images of antlered beasts on cave walls. Primitive hunters were admired not only for their ability to provide meat, but also for their skill in outwitting the biggest and best-antlered bulls and bucks. Today, modern hunters continue this ancient tradition, lured to fields and forests every fall by the spell of impressive antlers and the almost mystical beasts that grow them.

Whitetail antlers are like snowflakes; no two are exactly alike. Each is as unique as a human fingerprint, but a lot more interesting. An old buck can go from being bald-headed in March to having antlers with foot-long tines in September. His rack may be wide and tall, narrow and short, sport as few as 3 tines per side or as many as 20. Its bases may be as gnarled and bumpy as hackberry bark, its main beams as smooth as an icicle. But why? What makes one buck grow mediocre antlers while another produces a magnificent monument of bone?

What Makes a Trophy Buck?

Four major factors influence antler size: birth weight, nutrition, genetics and age. Hunters and biologists do not agree on the relative importance of each factor, nor do they fully understand how each interacts. Nevertheless, each plays a role in determining trophy potential.

BIRTH WEIGHT – Healthy, heavy does give birth to healthy, heavy fawns, and heavy male fawns generally grow into large-antlered bucks later in life. This robust health is a product of good nutrition. Thus, deer from overpopulated herds where quality forage is in short supply are born with one strike against them. If male fawns do not enjoy good nutrition from conception through their first year, they may never produce trophy antlers.

NUTRITION – Nutrition may play the most significant role in the development of both antlers and above-average body weight. If a buck is not getting enough high-quality forage, he simply can't maximize antler growth. In the George Reserve, a 1,146-acre fenced research area in Michigan, data were collected that demonstrate how buck weights compare to overall deer density, which in turn reflects forage quality. Bucks averaged 147 pounds when the population stood at about 126 animals (1941), 158 pounds when the herd was reduced to 67 deer (1958-1971) and 168 pounds when the population was lowered to 10 deer (1971-1975). As body size rose, so did antler size. Overall, racks were largest during 1971-1975, when bucks were heaviest.

A series of classic pre-World War II experiments done with red deer in Europe also supports the case for nutrition. Back then researchers noticed that red deer antlers collected in the area thousands of years earlier were much larger than contemporary racks. Could forage have been more nutritious back in the "good old days"? To find out, researchers fed stags highly nutritious supplemental diets including sesame seed oil mixed with various natural and agricultural plants. Forage was varied to encourage stags to consume large quantities.

The results were rather amazing. Of the 36 animals in the research project, 35 grew antlers that placed among the 100 best red deer antlers known. Six exceeded the then world record. Obviously, a highly nutritious diet was essential to growing huge red deer stags and antlers. The same is true of whitetails.

More recently, researchers at Mississippi State University purchased a 9-year-old buck that had been fed a low-protein, corn-only diet. The deer had relatively small, 8-point antlers that spread only 17 inches apart. The old deer was given a 16 percent protein diet, and bingo! Its next rack sported 21 points and a 27-inch spread. Not bad, considering the animal was well past its prime.

A Texas buck that has reached his full trophy potential

RESEARCH conducted at Mississippi State University shows that the saying, "Once a spike, always a spike," is false. The buck shown above, called "Timbuck," weighed 94 pounds and had antlers less than 2 inches long his first year (above). Four years later, after being fed a high-protein diet, Timbuck weighed 210 pounds and had an enormous 11-point rack (left). In fact, of the 18 spikes fed similar foods, the average-size buck at age 5½ carried a 10-point rack with a 17-inch inside spread.

For years, hunters have been arguing whether small-antlered bucks, especially those with only spike antlers, should be removed from herds to prevent them from siring more small-antlered bucks. Are these animals genetically inferior?

In 1973, Texas biologists began a major study looking at the interaction of nutrition and genetics on antler development. They showed a relationship between poor nutrition among yearling bucks and the formation of spike antlers. Young bucks on less than 8 percent protein developed small antlers, often spikes. The researchers subsequently fed nine yearling spike bucks high-protein diets and found that although their antlers did improve, they were smaller than those of similar-age bucks who started out with branched antlers rather than spikes. In fact, only 35 percent of the yearling spike bucks produced racks with eight points or more, while 95 percent of the yearling bucks with branched antlers went on to produce racks with eight points or more.

More recent studies done at Mississippi State University, however, tell a different story and demonstrate the importance of good nutrition on whitetail antler development. These studies show that small young bucks, including spike bucks, grow large antlers when given a high 13 to 16 percent protein diet (above). In a healthy deer herd, less than 25 percent of the yearling bucks will be spikes. In some high-density whitetail populations where the habitat has been overbrowsed, as many as 50 percent of all yearling bucks may be spikes. In low-density areas where more browse exists, only 3 percent of all yearling bucks may be spikes.

So what is the best management strategy for spike bucks – remove them or let them walk? Most biologists today believe that good nutrition from birth is the key to producing big antlers. If a deer manager wants to have more bucks with big antlers, his first step should be to provide good habitat with plenty of nutritious browse. When he designs his harvest strategy, he should take plenty of does to control the herd size and reduce demands on forage. At the same time, he should restrict buck harvest, even the harvest of spikes. The more well-fed bucks he has in the herd, the more trophies it will produce.

GENETICS – A buck's genes determine the shape and size of his antlers and the length of specific tines. It is possible to trace an unusual antler trait through several generations of bucks in an area. For example, a mature buck sporting wide beams with short tines may sire dozens of fawns that eventually grow wide, short-tined antlers of their own. This trait may persist for decades in one area while antlers that are narrow but extremely tall may be common in a herd a few miles away.

Some suggest that bucks with small antlers should be removed from a population in order to remove their "inferior" genes. However, research has proven that genetic potential cannot be determined by judging the antler size of yearling bucks. The advocates of culling also fail to recognize that does contribute half the genes to any buck fawn – and there is no way to tell what kind of antler genes a buck's mother carries.

In many states about 80 percent of all antlered bucks are harvested each year. Does this high buck harvest remove genes for large antlers and lead to smaller racks? There are no studies to show that this occurs. Even though the breeding bucks in these herds are very young, the genetically strongest are probably still most dominant and still sire most of the fawns.

Genetics are the most important factor in the growth of non-typical antlers. A buck often shows the same abnormal points on his antlers year after year. These abnormal points are usually genetically controlled, and they normally begin to show at 2½ or 3½ years of age. As the buck ages, even more abnormalities may develop.

AGE – A buck's body takes care of business before it indulges in frivolities like antlers. The growth of bone and muscle is always a top priority; antlers grow with the energy left over after the essentials are provided for. Since the average buck's body doesn't stop growing until 5 or 6 years of age, he can't grow his biggest antlers until then. All other factors being equal, a fully mature buck will produce a more impressive rack than an immature buck. Research suggests that some genetically superior bucks on high-protein diets can reach maximum body and antler size at age 4, but most don't peak until 6½ or 7½ years of age. Most bucks' racks begin to deteriorate in size after 7½ years of age, but they often become more palmated (right).

Old buck with palmated antlers

Trophy whitetail using a mineral lick

Improving Nutrition

While a buck's age and genetic makeup influence his antler growth, he'll never reach his full potential as a trophy without good nutrition. Whitetails require many nutrients, including calcium, phosphorus, sodium, potassium, iron, magnesium, other trace minerals, vitamins and amino acids. Calcium and phosphorus are especially important for antler growth and development. Research suggests that deer need diets of .15 to .30 percent phosphorus and .40 to .65 percent calcium.

Several livestock mineral blocks on the market contain nutrients (especially calcium and phosphorus) deer require (above). Some deer enthusiasts believe that whitetails using mineral licks grow more rapidly and produce heavier antlers than deer without licks, but studies don't always support their view. One 2-year study showed no positive results using mineral supplements in the wild. Where concentrations of natural minerals are low, bucks may get a boost in body and antler size from mineral supplements provided over a long period of time. In the end, though, the best way to keep bucks well fed and headed toward trophy status is to control deer populations.

Managing for Trophy Bucks

When the typical hunter steps into the deer woods on opening morning, he wants to kill a trophy buck. Game agencies and landowners often have a different agenda – they are generally more interested in a high harvest of females to control deer populations and reduce crop damage. A deer management scheme pioneered in the southern U.S. can take care of both demands. It's known as *Quality Deer Management* (QDM).

Quality Deer Management began in South Carolina but is now common throughout the South. The objective is to produce healthy deer and change hunter behavior at the same time. Here's how one manager used it in Colleton County, South Carolina:

After decades of bucks-only hunting, the county's deer herd was overwhelmed with does. Area biologist Joe Hamilton wanted to shoot more does, but he had trouble selling the idea. Hunters in the county had traditionally opposed shooting does. Hamilton explained that the harvest of a doe theoretically frees up enough browse to support an additional buck. He managed to get his additional doe permits, and, at the same time he increased the doe harvest, he asked hunters to avoid shooting yearling bucks and all fawns.

Such changes in hunting regime should have several effects on deer herds. The increased harvest of does should reduce the size of the herd by reducing its reproductive potential. Fewer deer mean more food and better nutrition for the deer that are left. Shooting more does should also increase the proportion of bucks in the herd. Protecting all fawns should have the same effect, since about half of all fawns are male. And if hunters pass up small bucks, more of the youngsters will survive to potential trophy age. The bottom line is healthier deer, healthier forage and more big bucks.

An ongoing study at Mississippi State University helps clarify QDM's potential for increasing the number and size of bucks in a whitetail herd. Researchers at Mississippi State found that only 1.6 percent of $1\frac{1}{2}$-year-old bucks and 4.4 percent of $2\frac{1}{2}$-year-olds in Mississippi die of natural causes. When a Mississippi hunter passes up a yearling buck, the buck is likely to survive another year, and he'll be bigger when the next hunting season arrives. This pattern isn't so pronounced in the North, where winters are harsh and more bucks die at an early age, but even in cold climates, QDM can boost the number of older bucks a whitetail herd produces.

To be most effective, QDM should be applied over an area of at least 2500 acres for a period of at least

A young bowhunter with an adult doe

5 years. Most properties are well under this minimum size, but there are still ways to establish a QDM effort. The key is forming a coalition of interested private landowners or hunting clubs. Once people understand the benefits of the QDM approach, it's not that hard to take cooperative action on large tracts of habitat controlled by several owners.

Let's consider a 1,000-acre farm with enough quality deer habitat to support about 50 healthy deer. Let's further assume that the sex ratio of deer on the farm is 1 buck to 6 does (which isn't unreasonable). This means the farm has about 7 bucks and 43 does. If we increase the doe harvest so the sex ratio becomes 1:1, we will have 25 bucks and 25 does on the same range, which is 18 more bucks than when we started QDM. If we further limit the harvest of all small bucks, then we will have many more large, mature bucks living on the farm as well.

One problem in implementing QDM in the North is that wildlife agencies in this region may not issue enough doe permits to bring sex ratios into balance. In these situations, implementing QDM is difficult. A club can ask its bowhunters to harvest females, and it can ask that all gun hunters secure doe permits. Even so, with higher restrictions on doe harvests in the North as compared to the southern United States, private deer managers may have trouble implementing QDM. For more information, write: Quality Deer Management Association, P.O. Box 707, Walterboro, SC 29488.

How Trophy Bucks Survive

Bucks, especially big bucks, are very secretive animals. Older bucks commonly live near people, yet they are almost never seen. We know bucks become more nocturnal as they age, so it's not too surprising that trophy bucks are so elusive. Some suggest that such big bucks leave an area when disturbance increases, but that seems unlikely – one study found that a density of 1 hunter per 10 acres did not force bucks to abandon their normal haunts.

A 1995 Texas study considered the way whitetail bucks react to human disturbance. The study showed that bucks were less flighty as they got older. Middle-aged bucks from $3^1/2$ to $4^1/2$ years old traveled farthest when spooked; bucks over $7^1/2$ years of age traveled the shortest distance. This research confirms what most experienced whitetail hunters already know – a big buck is secure in his home range. He's learned that slow, deliberate movements away from potential danger work better than a long, panic-stricken run.

Bucks that survive to old age are cagey about the bedding areas they select, too. In skimpy cover like the farm country of the Midwest, bucks may travel several miles from choice nighttime feeding areas to the dense cover where they bed down during the day. In the South's extensive timber plantations, good cover and browse are nearly always close together, so bucks don't have to travel as far between forage and secure bedding areas.

A pregnant doe eats for herself and her unborn fawn in the spring, so she often generally beds close to prime feeding areas and maximizes her chow time. For this reason, it's not unusual to see does in strips of cover near farming operations. Trophy bucks aren't as desperate for food and often prefer to bed as far as they can get from human disturbance. This may leave them far from the best feed. Some biologists suggest that this habit may have evolutionary value. The mature buck may leave the best feed to his does so that his offspring are born healthy and vigorous, preserving his genes in the next generation. As the summer progresses, a buck's antlers and body begin to demand more energy and he may move into prime feeding areas nearer the does.

Trophy bucks spend much of their time in impenetrable cover. These areas provide bucks with such dependable sanctuary that they often use them as bedding sites for months, even years. Often as small as 1 to 2 acres, these refuges provide the buck with the cover he needs to hide during the day and ready access to nearby feeding areas at night.

In the South, these hideouts are often in swamps. In the Northwest, they may be impenetrable willow thickets next to a major river, positioned so that prevailing winds allow safe ingress and egress. In the North, they may be thick conifer stands; hawthorn thickets; abandoned fields with dense tangles of sumac, prickly ash or aspen or a combination thereof. During the rut the trails to and from these bedding sites will be marked with many rubs. The bedding area itself will have some major rubs, perhaps a scrape and lots of deer pellets in a small area.

Big City Bucks

As suburbs have crept into the countryside, as more and more people have built homes in the heart of deer habitat, whitetails have adapted to city life. In fact, urban deer populations may contain more big bucks than herds in more traditional deer habitat. Large homes built on several acres are often closed to hunting. Deer thrive in these situations as long as there is cover, some browse and good bedding sites. With little or no hunting, good food and cover, bucks grow to older ages and trophy size.

In many of these areas, whitetail populations get out of hand. Householders who started out with an affection for the brown-eyed doe in the backyard often change their minds when hoards of deer eat every shrub, flower and vegetable on the property. Whitetails are hosts to Lyme disease, a serious human ailment, and collisions between deer and autos are costly and potentially dangerous. More and more communities are facing the problem of too many deer (p. 29).

One solution to the urban deer problem is to allow bowhunting in town. Bowhunting poses few hazards to hunters or nearby nonhunters; it's quiet and unobtrusive, and it can control a deer population.

Of course, getting permission to hunt is important for any deer hunter, but it's absolutely critical for the urban hunter. In many eastern communities with urban deer problems, groups of experienced, ethical bowhunters have formed informal clubs that landowners and home owners can contact when they want deer removed.

These clubs have membership qualifications and ethics rules that are strictly enforced. Members must meet with landowners and become acquainted with their concerns.

Once a bowhunter has permission to hunt in a suburb, he should make an extraordinary effort to keep landowners in the area happy. If he arrives before daylight, he should avoid making noise that might disturb the residents. He should do his best to maintain a friendly one-to-one relationship with people in the neighborhood. A little courtesy helps keep the backyards open for hunting the next fall.

Municipalities initiate controlled bowhunts to reduce deer numbers. That means harvesting female deer is critical. While most hunters want to kill bucks, they will do more to control the herd by taking does. Once the meat gets to the table, nobody will know the difference. Of course, when that once-in-a-lifetime trophy walks into range, there's generally time to make an exception.

A bowhunter in the suburbs can better his chances by hunting strips of timber (the thicker the cover, the better) used as travel corridors by deer. Heavily used trails, lines of tree rubs and scrapes during the fall rut mark these corridors. A hunter using a stand should get settled well before daylight to avoid disturbing deer moving through the corridors to their bedding sites in early morning. It's smart to approach the stand from a different direction each day to disperse human scent and prevent deer from identifying a pattern of human use.

State	Typical	Non-typical	Total
Kansas	33	22	55
Illinois	33	18	51
Iowa	37	13	50
Minnesota	16	11	27
Wisconsin	11	5	16
Ohio	10	3	13
Indiana	6	4	10
Nebraska	5	5	10
Missouri	6	2	8
Kentucky	3	4	7

THE TOP TEN PLACES where bowhunters have taken trophy bucks scoring at least 170 typical points and 195 non-typical points are shown above (see p. 90 to learn how antlers are scored). Though Montana, Saskatchewan, Alberta and Manitoba don't make the list, this probably reflects the low hunting pressure that occurred there until recently. Watch for these areas to show dramatic increases in the numbers of trophies harvested in the years to come.

Where to Find Trophy Bucks

Whitetails in the northern United States and Canada have larger bodies than those farther south. But do larger-bodied bucks have larger antlers? Although there are exceptions, the answer is generally "yes." Also, whitetail racks tend to get larger in the Midwest than in the East. When it comes to the potential for growing trophy antlers, bucks in the Midwest have three advantages over their eastern brethren. First: the soils in the Midwest are exceptionally fertile, so forage is exceptionally abundant and nutritious. Second: when it comes to intimidating rival bucks, a large rack may be more useful in the relatively open habitat of the Midwest than in the thickets of the East, simply because midwestern bucks can see each other better. Third: large antlers certainly make movement through the East's dense cover more difficult. And as a result, small-antlered bucks may have evolved as better suited for the habitat than large-antlered animals.

A 1994 University of Georgia study considered variables that were correlated with bucks listed in the Boone and Crockett record book. It showed that the number of big bucks harvested in an area increased with the total amount of farmland and the amount of land left idle. The number of trophy bucks also went up with the amount of corn, soybeans, alfalfa and oats planted. In addition, there were fewer big bucks harvested in states where deer densities were over 30 deer per square mile. There was another negative correlation – states with higher average rainfall tended to have fewer record-book listings. The bottom line? The farm country of the prairies is prime trophy habitat.

Several states consistently produce record-book-size bucks (left). Of these states, the three top producers for trophies shot by bow and arrow are Kansas, Illinois and Iowa.

In the past two decades there has been an increase in the number of trophies taken in Montana, Texas, Saskatchewan, Alberta and Manitoba. The circumstances surrounding Montana whitetails is unusual. Whitetail herds in eastern Montana have expanded their range along river bottoms and are thriving in this habitat. They have good forage, dense cover and face limited hunting pressure, so a high proportion of bucks reach older trophy ages.

In Texas, there are more trophy deer than ever, due in large part to the aggressive deer management strategies implemented by private ranches. The most common of these practices include supplemental feeding programs and the protection of immature bucks.

Saskatchewan, Alberta and Manitoba have always had some big whitetails, but they were in remote areas not heavily hunted. The growing demand for big bucks combined with the development of more effective hunting techniques has heightened demand for Canadian whitetails. Canadian outfitters are beginning to recognize the value of their trophy bucks and are working harder to offer whitetail hunts to hunters from the United States.

Trophy hunting has drawn increasing criticism over the last 20 years. Antihunters and many nonhunters view trophy hunting as the wasteful slaughter of prime big game animals for nothing but their antlers. In reality, nothing could be further from the truth.

Most trophy hunters follow a stringent ethical code. How the hunter conducts him/herself; the experience of the hunt; the thoughts about the unseen, large animal that is living in the hunting area . . . these things are more important to the ethical trophy hunter than success or the size of a set of antlers. The trophy hunter of the past and the trophy hunter of today share a reverence for the great stag, the eternal embodiment of strength, grace and intelligence – the soul of American wilderness.

Field-Judging Trophies

You don't have to be a trophy hunter to enjoy estimating the size of antlers when in the field. While the process of field-judging may seem complicated at first, after a little practice you'll soon be an expert.

The Boone and Crockett Club maintains records for trophy bucks that are "picked up" (meaning that the antlers weren't from a hunter-killed trophy) and those taken by either gun or bow. The Pope and Young Club keeps similar records, but only for bucks taken by bow. The Boone and Crockett scoring system is used by both clubs to measure a buck's antlers. Both organizations have minimum-size requirements for entry, with those of the B & C Club being much higher: B & C – typical, 170 points, non-typical, 195; P & Y – typical, 125, non-typical, 150.

Interest in these clubs and entries into both record books are growing dramatically. Some state game agencies also keep records of trophy deer. And during the off-season, whitetail shows exhibiting these trophy-sized racks are gaining in popularity throughout North America.

How Trophy Bucks Are Scored

Of course, a trophy is in the eye of the beholder. However, when it comes to whitetail bucks, most hunters limit the use of this term to bucks that have at least one antler with four points, or tines, and a decent inside spread.

While the average hunter chooses his/her own standard for what may qualify as a trophy, this level usually is close to the 125-point minimum required for entry in the P & Y typical category.

The B & C scoring system is based on the following factors: main beam length, number and length of tines, circumference along the main beam, inside spread and symmetry between the antlers. Of all of the factors, the number of points is probably the most important for a high score. For example, while many bucks make the P & Y book with four points on each antler (called a four-by-four), only a small percentage of these score high enough for the B & C book.

Non-typicals are scored the same as typicals, but instead of deducting for abnormal points, these are *added* to the final score. An example of a completed scoring form is shown on the opposite page. Hunters wishing to purchase a detailed guide (right) on how to measure whitetails can write: Pope and Young Club, Box 548, Chatfield, MN 55923.

How to Field-Judge Whitetails

Many bowhunters dream of shooting a buck that qualifies for the P & Y record book. For them, quick and accurate field-judging is a must so they don't release an arrow on a smaller buck. The easiest way to field-judge a buck's antlers is to estimate them against those body features that have a known length (opposite page).

Serious hunters practice their field-judging skills year-round so they are prepared when a potential trophy presents himself during the season. One of the best ways to practice is to attend a whitetail show in your area. As you walk down the aisles admiring the trophy heads on display, stop 15 to 25 yards away from a mount and guess its score. For the first dozen or so heads, mentally keep track as you add the various antler measurements. When you come up with a final score, walk up to the mount and check its official score. Your ultimate goal is to guess the final score within about 5 points with only a quick glance. After all, bucks in the wild won't stand around waiting for you to add and subtract.

FIELD-JUDGING bucks in the wild usually must be done with a quick glance. The 8-point typical buck shown above scores about 125 points.

Field-judging Tips

NUMBER OF POINTS. Few bucks ever qualify for P & Y with less than four points on each antler. The quickest way to count the number of total points on an antler is by checking the points projecting off the main beam (called *points up*) when viewed broadside. Don't worry about the brow tine and tip of the antler; just add them later. For example, a 6-point buck (left) has one point up; an 8-pointer (middle), two up; a 10-pointer (right), three up. But just because a buck has four points per antler does not mean he will easily make the record book. Any deductions for asymmetry may cause a smaller "four-by-four" to drop below the minimum.

INSIDE SPREAD. The spread, ear to ear, for an alert buck is 16 to 18 inches. Most bucks need at least a 16-inch spread to make the P & Y record book. Although a few bucks with 12- or 13-inch inside spreads qualify as trophies, they must sport very long tines, be almost perfectly symmetrical and have long, thick main beams.

TINE LENGTH. A P & Y trophy buck should have at least two points on each antler that are 6 inches long or longer. Since a deer's ear is 6 to 8 inches long, that can be used for estimation.

MAIN BEAM LENGTH. An antler that curves in at the tip rather than staying straight indicates a long main beam. The rule of thumb in the field is that a main beam must have at least 6 inches of antler bent inward at the tip. Total main beam length for P & Y consideration should be at least 19 inches; B & C, 24 inches.

MASS (circumference along the main beam). While mass is not a critical factor for a buck to score 125 points, it is very important for bucks to exceed the B & C record book minimum of 170 points. Mass can be estimated by using the circumference of the eye, which is about 4 inches, as a comparison.

Index

Contributing Photographers (Note: T=*Top*, C=*Center*, B=*Bottom*, L=*Left*, R=*Right*, I=*Inset*)

Charles J. Alsheimer
Bath, New York
©*Charles J. Alsheimer pp. cover The
Complete Hunter, 10TL, 13BR, 16BR, 17CL,
17BL, 19B, 20R, 33B, 34TR, 54R, 61TL,
61TR, 73, 85R, 86, 90T*

Mike Biggs
Fort Worth, Texas
©*Mike Biggs pp. 15L, 16T, 18, 35T, 35I, 44T,
49BC, 53, 64, 68T, 78*

Denver Bryan
Bozeman, Montana
©*Denver Bryan pp. 14TR, 22T, 50-51,
77, 92T*

Gary Clancy
Byron, Minnesota
©*Gary Clancy pp. 16BL, 43*

Daniel J. Cox
Bozeman, Montana
©*Daniel J. Cox pp. 32-33T, 62T*

Jeanne Drake
Las Vegas, Nevada
©*Jeanne Drake pp. 39B, 93TR*

J. Faircloth
Charlotte, North Carolina
©*J. Faircloth p. 34BR*

D. Robert Franz
Morrison, Colorado
©*D. Robert Franz pp. 9L, 11B*

The Green Agency
Belgrade, Montana
©*Rich Kirchner p. 10BL*

Harry A. Jacobson
Mississippi State, Mississippi
©*Harry Jacobson p. 84L, 84R*

Donald M. Jones
Troy, Michigan
©*Donald M. Jones pp. 4, 8, 10BR, 13T, 14TL,
14TC, 14BR, 17BR, 20L, 24-25, 31T, 36-37,
38, 48BL, 54L, 62-63, 65T, 66, 68B, 80-81, 88*

Bill Kinney
Ridgeland, Wisconsin
©*Bill Kinney pp. 6-7, 10CL, 10TR, 14BL, 41,
48TR, 49BL, 70, 72T, 72B, 76, 85L, 88*

Lance Krueger
McAllen, Texas
©*Lance Krueger pp. 14BC, 49TL, 49TC, 49BR,
55T, 55C, 55B, 60, 65B, 83, 92BL, 92BC, 93BR*

Claudine Laabs
West Palm Beach, Florida
©*Claudine Laabs p. 13I*

Lon E. Lauber
Wasilla, Alaska
©*Lon E. Lauber p. 9R*

Bill Lea
Franklin, North Carolina
©*Bill Lea pp. cover The Complete
Bowhunter, 32B, 34L*

Steve Maas
East Bethel, Minnesota
©*Steve Maas pp. 8I, 11T*

Bill Marchel
Fort Ripley, Minnesota
©*Bill Marchel pp. 22B, 30, 44B, 47, 49TR,
52, 56-57, 59, 67, 73I, 87, 92BR, 93TL*

Minnesota Historical Society
St. Paul, Minnesota
©*S.A. Johnson, Phillips pp. 26-27*

Janice Ozoga
Munising, Michigan
©*Janice Ozoga p. 12*

Ted Rose
North Manchester, Indiana
©*Ted Rose pp. 15R, 93BL*

Daniel Snyder
Rivesville, West Virginia
©*Daniel Snyder p. 2*

Bob Zaiglin
Uvalde, Texas
©*Bob Zaiglin p. 69*

Cowles Creative Publishing offers a variety of how-to books. For information write:

　　Cowles Creative Publishing Subscriber Books
　　5900 Green Oak Drive
　　Minnetonka, MN 55343

Other outdoor books available from the publisher: *The Art of Freshwater Fishing, Cleaning & Cooking Fish, Fishing With Live Bait, Largemouth Bass, Panfish, The Art of Hunting, Fishing With Artificial Lures, Walleye, Smallmouth Bass, Dressing & Cooking Wild Game, Freshwater Gamefish of North America, Trout, Secrets of the Fishing Pros, Fishing Rivers & Streams, Fishing Tips & Tricks, Fishing Natural Lakes, White-tailed Deer, Northern Pike & Muskie, America's Favorite Fish Recipes, Fishing Man-made Lakes, The Art of Fly Tying, America's Favorite Wild Game Recipes, Advanced Bass Fishing, Upland Game Birds, North American Game Animals, North American Game Birds, Advanced Whitetail Hunting, Fly-Fishing Equipment & Skills, Fly Fishing for Trout in Streams–Subsurface Techniques, Fly-Tying Techniques & Patterns, Fly Rod Gamefish–The Freshwater Species*